P9-EDU-891

THE WOMAN QUESTION

THE WOMAN QUESTION
Defining Voices, 1837–1883

Volume I of
THE WOMAN QUESTION
Society and Literature in
Britain and America, 1837–1883

Elizabeth K. Helsinger
Robin Lauterbach Sheets
William Veeder

GARLAND PUBLISHING, INC • NEW YORK & LONDON
1983

© 1983 Elizabeth K. Helsinger, Robin Lauterbach Sheets, and William Veeder
All rights reserved

Library of Congress Cataloging in Publication Data

Helsinger, Elizabeth K., 1943–
  The woman question.

  Includes bibliographical references and index.
  Contents: v. 1. Defining voices—v. 2. Social
issues—v. 3. Literary issues.
    1. Women—England—History—19th century—Collected
works. 2. Women—United States—History—19th century—
Collected works. 3. Women in literature—England—His-
tory—19th century—Collected works. 4. Women in
literature—United States—History—19th century—
Collected works. 5. Feminism—England—History—19th
century—Collected works. 6. Feminism—United States—
History—19th century—Collected works. I. Sheets,
Robin Ann. II. Veeder, William R. III. Title.
HQ1599.E5H44 1983   305.4′0942   80-9040
ISBN 0-8240-9301-1 (v. 1)

HQ
1599
.E5
H44
1983
V.1

39, 741

Printed on acid-free, 250-year-life paper
Manufactured in the United States of America

Acknowledgments

In the eight years since this project was conceived we have accumulated many debts. In particular we would like to thank Nina Auerbach, Edy Cobey, Donald W. Dayton, Michael P. Ditchkofsky, T.J. Edelstein, Clarissa Erwin, Mary Anne Ferguson, Robert Ferguson, Dan Gottlieb, John S. and Robin Haller, Sally Hoffheimer, Randolph Woods Ivy, Robin Jacoby, Elizabeth Janeway, U.C. Knoepflmacher, Margaret Lourie, Ann Matthews, Katharine Rogers, Sue Sayne, Joanne Schlichter, Kitty Von Pabst, George Worth, John Wright, Bonnie Zimmerman, the Humanities Division of the University of Chicago, the Taft Foundation, and the University of Cincinnati Research Council.

We are grateful to the following for permission to reproduce works in their collections: *Forbes Magazine* Collection (illustration 1, Volume I; illustration 2, Volume II); The Tate Gallery, London (illustration 5, Volume III); The Metropolitan Museum of Art, Rogers Fund, 1908 (illustration 7, Volume III). For permission to reprint material from previously published works we wish to thank: Harvard University Press and Manchester University Press for excerpts from *The Letters of Elizabeth Gaskell*, edited by J.A.V. Chapple and Arthur Pollard; University of California Press for a passage quoted in *Christina Rossetti*, by Lona M. Packer; Yale University Library and Yale University Press for a Barbara Bodichon letter included in *The George Eliot Letters*, edited by Gordon Haight. We have made every effort to identify the owners of copyrighted material; we would appreciate having any oversights called to our attention.

Finally, to our spouses, Howard and Jim and Mary, to the three children who have grown up with this project, Aaron and

CAMROSE LUTHERAN COLLEGE
LIBRARY

Sarah and Maisie, and to the three children who were born while it was underway, the two Alex's and Willy, we owe thanks for their respective patience or joyful obliviousness to our long and often perplexed encounter with the Victorian Woman Question.

Illustrations

Contents

Introduction

Discoveries about Victorian women have within the last decade raised serious doubts about our modern understanding of the nineteenth century. What really were the culture's attitudes toward men and women? The question is much less easy to answer now than it once seemed to be. Close study of public opinion between 1837 and 1883 suggests that the traditional model of "a" Victorian attitude—patriarchal domination, expressed publicly as "woman worship"—is inadequate. The predominant form of Victorian writing about women is not pronouncement but debate. Moreover, the arguments in this debate were both more complex and more fluid than the model of a single dominant cultural myth would indicate. For Victorians of "the articulate classes,"[1] the Woman Question, as they themselves called it, really was a question.

Almost any public statement bearing on the Woman Question —whether an essay, a review, a novel, a poem, a lecture, a cartoon, or a painting—was likely to generate a chain of responses, and to be read as a response to prior statements in an ongoing public discussion. To view any of these statements out of context, which as modern readers we often do when we study a novel or a painting, may properly emphasize the integrity of imaginative creation but can only distort our perception of Victorian thinking about women. Charlotte Brontë, Elizabeth Cady Stanton, and John Stuart Mill were not isolated dissenters from a chorus praising one womanly ideal. The controversies in which Brontë, Stanton, and Mill participated form the context for prescriptive writers like Sarah Ellis and Anthony Comstock. Until we understand how these voices of protest and prescription relate to the larger contemporary discussion, the old concept of a single public Victorian attitude toward women will remain largely intact.

For the present study, we have reconstructed the debate which surrounds prescriptive pronouncements, protests, and imaginative literature about women. Though many of the voices are no longer familiar, most were regular or momentarily prominent contributors to the public discourse of their time. Some are close to the centers of a literate, governing, and opinion-shaping class; others are more eccentric. All, however, were responding to one another in public forums—in books and pamphlets, from pulpits and lecterns, and above all, through the periodicals. For the most part, these exchanges did not take place on a high theoretical plane; they were precipitated by particular political, economic, scientific, religious, or cultural events, and they focused on specific and limited problems. Should married women be granted property rights? What can be done about the high infant mortality rate among mothers working in the mills? What do physiological studies of evolutionary man indicate about women's mental capacities? Does the popularity of sensation novels reveal suppressed anti-social impulses among female readers? Nearly every contemporary topic provoked controversy over women, but the diversity of opinions and issues should not obscure the crucial point: for literate Anglo-American Victorians, woman's nature and place were called into question.

To convey the special qualities of the Victorian debate we have departed in several ways from both the normal format (the anthology or collection of documents) and the prevailing approaches of recent work on the Woman Question. We wish to preserve the polemical immediacy of public controversy by letting the Victorians speak for themselves in the give-and-take of the original debate. At the same time, however, particular voices and controversies need to be placed within their social and cultural context. Our book is thus a critical history of controversies presented directly through Victorian speakers. We have varied the proportions of text and analysis from chapter to chapter. Where the intrinsic interest of the texts is great, especially if they are unfamiliar today, we have quoted generously; in other cases we have excerpted more sparingly and expanded our historical and critical commentary. To include some forgotten writers important in their own day we have omitted sustained analysis of others, like Mary Wollstonecraft, whose work is better known and more accessible today.

We have also departed from prevailing practice by considering British and American discussions together as parts of a single debate. On some issues, of course, the discussions are simply parallel, while others diverge to follow national or local concerns. Nonetheless, Victorian Britain and America formed a single community of letters, within which national variations in the treatment of women provided yet another subject for common discussion. Our writers constantly refer to, quote, and directly respond to statements of conditions from across the Atlantic. Though we have not attempted a comprehensive comparison of British and American views, we have included numerous instances of cross-Atlantic exchanges, and noted parallels and divergences of opinion in particular controversies. Where it became necessary to choose between British and American versions of a debate, we have given the one less familiar today, usually the British—except where the American controversy was notably more heated (as in the case of most religious issues). Our Anglo-American perspective affirms for the Woman Question as a whole what Mary Macarthur observed of the womens' trade union leagues: that the British movement was both the grandmother and the granddaughter of the American.[2]

Finally, our treatment of the Woman Question departs from much recent practice by focusing on middle-class opinions and including male as well as female voices. These choices reflect the nature of the public debate: it was a largely middle-class discussion in which both men and women participated. We have not set out to uncover new examples of the lost views of working class or female sub-cultures. We have, however, made extensive use of the work of feminist critics and social historians who have explored these hidden strains of behavior and opinion. As far as possible, we have tried to indicate the distance between those perceptions of women which shaped the public debate, and evidence which suggests a different Victorian reality. Our aim is to study the nature of that distance and, wherever possible, to examine the reasons for it: personal, social, and cultural. However, this should not suggest that public perception was always at odds with private practice and belief. Conflicting opinions and competing mythologies did find expression within the public debate. Moreover, those who defended "woman's place" and those who sympathized with women's rights were often far more closely linked than we had suspected.

It is, indeed, often difficult to predict where the "conservative" and "dissenting" positions will lie in any particular controversy—or to predict just which assumptions about woman's nature conservatives or dissenters will employ in their arguments. Relatively few Victorians maintained rigidly consistent theoretical positions. Many of the most outspoken, like Elizabeth Cady Stanton, could appeal—with equal conviction and in the same speech—to conflicting cultural myths about women. And even those who were theoretically consistent might still disagree over practical applications: whether, for example, women should be doctors. Conversely, defenders of women doctors might make different assumptions about women's intellectual abilities, rights to professional training, or special feminine characteristics (like patience and solicitude) which fitted them for medicine. Such diversity of both argument and conclusion makes any strict definition of feminist or anti-feminist positions very difficult. We can speak more accurately not of positions but of a set of competing, though not mutually exclusive, myths or models for woman's place in society. Controversialists used these myths to argue for opposing solutions to contemporary problems.

Among such myths we have found four which are especially pervasive. First, the familiar Angel in the House—the wife and mother described in Sarah Ellis' conduct manuals, praised in Felicia Heman's poetry, and embodied in the Agnes Wickfield of Dickens' *David Copperfield*. Her nature is loving and self-sacrificing; her responsibilities, domestic and maternal. Although she is a delicate creature worshipped and protected by husbands and sons, she not only works hard at home but also provides continuity and moral strength in a rapidly changing society. Second, the model of complete equality—women as equal contracting partners with men, legally, sexually, and economically free agents in both domestic and professional matters. Though this model had some famous and articulate advocates—Mill, William Thompson, George Drysdale, Susan B. Anthony—it was so disconcertingly radical and so much at odds with the widespread interest in woman's "special" nature and duties that it seems to have played a smaller role in the public debate than two other competitors to the angelic ideal. One of these might be called the Angel out of the House. Although this model for woman's behavior accepted fundamental differences between men and women, it extended the wife's sphere beyond her home and family. The Angel out of the House did not challenge the leadership of men, but she did define her own distinctive tasks, ministering to the needs of the world at large through philanthropy or social service. The incarnation of this freed Angel, in the popular view, was Florence Nightingale. Finally, there is a radical version of the angelic ideal which combines a belief in woman's distinctive nature with claims for a leadership role in the world—a female saviour leading the way to a fuller humanity and ushering in a new era of community and love. This vision of woman's unique role, which might best be described as apocalyptic feminism, attracted both eccentrics like Eliza Farnham and, to some extent, even staunch conservatives like Sara Josepha Hale, editor of *Godey's Lady's Magazine*. For some, like Farnham, it amounted to an absolute claim to female superiority; for others, like Margaret Fuller, a temporary claim for woman's special role within an overall vision of human equality. Though this view of woman, like the egalitarian view, was held by a minority, it affected surprisingly large numbers of women, especially in America. In the last third of the century it helped fuel the campaigns to abolish contagious diseases acts, hold men to a single sexual standard, promote temperance, improve prisons, and reform corrupt municipal governments. The distinctions between the Angel in the House, the Angel out of the House, and the Female Saviour are often particularly difficult to draw. One or more of these three related but competing myths of woman underlie most of the arguments brought forward in the Woman Question.

These alternative views of woman have, of course, relatives and antecedents before 1837. The Victorian Woman Question is only one chapter in the history of that debate. Both the advocates of an angelic ideal and, particularly, the advocates of equality have important predecessors among late eighteenth and early nineteenth-century writers. Many of the particular issues debated by Victorians had also been discussed before. Yet Victorians themselves, beyond a rare reference to blue stockings or Mary Wollstonecraft, or to early female preachers and writers, did not often trace their views back to the immediate past. To some extent they were right: distinctive emphases, particular myths, even a common set of terms—"woman's mission," "woman's sphere," "woman's influence"—unite the varied controversies between the 1830s and the 1880s.

We have begun our history with six chapters which illustrate the particularly Victorian qualities of the debate. Volume I: *Defining Voices* is exemplary rather than historical; it focuses on representative texts, figures, and controversies for what they reveal about the general character of the Woman Question rather than for their historical connections with earlier and later phases of the debate. Sarah Lewis' *Woman's Mission*, William Thompson's *Appeal of One Half the Human Race*, and Margaret Fuller's *Woman in the Nineteenth Century*—three texts from the second quarter of the century—define the myths and establish the vocabulary of the Angel, the egalitarian ideal, and the Female Saviour. The next three chapters exemplify the private and public debate to which conflicting myths inevitably led. For the private side we have chosen Victoria herself; the Queen strikingly reflects the anxieties and contradictions of the age named for her. Two popular texts from the 1860s, John Ruskin's "Of Queens' Gardens" and Eliza Lynn Linton's "The Girl of the Period," illustrate how the Woman Question typically interacted with contemporary social and cultural concerns to generate public controversy. The second and third volumes of our study reconstruct and analyze the debate in society and literature as it evolved across the half century from Victoria's accession to the mid-1880s. Volume II: *Social Issues* traces the progress of controversy in law, science, work, and religion. Volume III: *Literary Issues* follows literary debates over the same period, dealing first with public discussion of the woman writer and second with the debate generated by a variety of literary heroines.

One last word. The authors of this history have sometimes found themselves in no more agreement than their Victorian subjects. On most matters our discussions have led to consensus, but we realize that our individual perceptions and myths—like those of the Victorians—run deep, and will be reflected in the selection of voices as well as in the commentary on them. The structure, the format, and the emphases on common themes and arguments are our joint decisions, but each chapter is the work of a single author. Some differences in attitude between them we have not attempted to resolve. Many of the questions debated in the nineteenth century are still very much alive. We can only offer our own differences as testimony to the continuing vitality of the debate.

Notes

¹So named by G.M. Young, *Victorian England: Portrait of an Age* (London: Oxford Univ. Press, 1936), p. 6.

²At the 1919 Convention of the National Women's Trade Union League of America, quoted by Gladys Boone in *The Women's Trade Union League in Great Britain and the United States of America* (New York: Columbia Univ. Press, 1942), p. 20.

The Woman Question
DEFINING VOICES
1837–1883

1

Sarah Lewis and Woman's Mission

In 1840, George Eliot wrote to her former schoolmistress, "Do recommend to all your married friends 'Woman's Mission' a 3.6d book and one you would like to read; the most philosophical and masterly on the subject I ever read or glanced over."[1] Published anonymously in 1839 by "an English lady, residing near London"[2] and subsequently attributed to Sarah Lewis, *Woman's Mission* was based on the work of one of Rousseau's most enthusiastic disciples, Louis Aimé Martin. In preparing Martin's influential book *De l'éducation des mères de famille, ou la civilisation du genre humain par les femmes* (1834) for an English audience, Lewis translated some passages directly, discarded those sections which dealt entirely with French morals and manners, and developed ideas which had long occupied her own mind.[3] Although George Eliot soon turned to the French source and found it to be "the real Greece whence Woman's Mission has only imported to us a few marbles,"[4] most readers were content with Lewis' immensely popular adaptation. *Woman's Mission* reflects ideas that are considered "Victorian" today but that were in fact present in America and England at least a quarter century before the young Queen's accession.[5]

In both countries, women's involvement in political and philanthropic activities provoked debate about their proper mission. Inspired by the evangelical revival, British and American women were working to improve prison conditions, curtail the use of alcohol, bring an end to prostitution, and abolish slavery. In the northeastern United States, women's efforts to free the blacks were especially important. In 1833 William Lloyd Garrison urged American women to follow the example of Amelia Opie and other British abolitionists who had deluged Parliament with antislavery petitions.[6] By petitioning, sponsoring fairs to raise funds, writing, and lecturing, women such as Lydia Maria Child, Maria Weston Chapman, and Angelina and Sarah Grimké established solidarity and gained the practical expertise necessary for later stages of the women's movement.

Although the actual campaign for female suffrage did not get under way until the 1848 Seneca Falls Convention, women abolitionists, were asserting their right to engage in political activity by speaking in public and by participating in antislavery societies. The first Anti-Slavery Convention of American Women passed an 1837 resolution that was radical in its redefinition of woman's sphere and in its claim for moral equality under God:

> Resolved, that as certain rights and duties are common to all moral beings, the time has come for woman to move in that sphere which Providence has assigned her, and no longer remain satisfied in the circumscribed limits which corrupt custom and a perverted application of Scripture have encircled her.[7]

Confronted with serious opposition from clerics and other abolitionists, women who lectured for the slave's cause were often forced to recognize, and then decry, the limitations of their own lives. In 1837, a highly critical pastoral letter written by Rev. Nehemiah Adams and approved by the Congregational Churches of Massachusetts prompted the brilliant speaker Sarah Grimké to issue her *Letters on the Equality of the Sexes and the Condition of Women*, a strong statement of women's grievances and a scriptural defense of equality.[8]

In England issues of women's rights and duties had also aroused public interest. As the *Westminster Review* said, "It is evident, from the number of works that have recently appeared entitled, or addressed to 'woman' that the situation of women, is at this moment, a matter of interest and discussion, especially to themselves."[9] When Victoria came to the throne in 1837, the decade gave little promise of improved political standing for her female subjects. Members of Parliament refused to consider an 1832 petition for women's suffrage, and in 1835 they greeted a proposal that women be allowed to watch parliamentary proceedings from a special gallery with ribald humor and occasional flashes of acrimony. More serious arguments for women's rights were, however, being presented in meeting halls and key periodicals. The Benthamites and Owenists had been concerned with women's suffrage for some time. William Thompson argued for enfranchisement in his *Appeal of One Half the Human Race* in 1825; *Westminster Review* took up the cause in 1829; and during the 1830s, the *Monthly Repository* and the *Metropolitan Magazine* continued to question women's exclusion from political rights and responsibilities. The Chartists supported women's suffrage in the original draft of their 1838 charter, and in 1839 the Female Political Union of Newcastle called upon fellow countrywomen to join the campaign.[10] Harriet Martineau praised the courage and intelligence of the American women abolitionists in an 1838 essay,[11] while Caroline Norton showed that an Englishwoman could alter the course of legislation: the 1839 Infants and Child Custody Bill she helped to pass was the first successful challenge to England's patriarchal legal system.

Woman's Mission was a moderate response to the situation, neither as reactionary as *Woman As She Is and As She Should Be* (1835), with its assumption of female inferiority, nor as radical as Harriet Martineau's *Society in America* (1837), with its indictment of female oppression. Women's involvement in philanthropy and their talk of political rights clearly made Sarah Lewis uneasy. But if her text is an argument against political equality, it is also a celebration of what she regards as woman's newly exalted position. Looking back to the eighteenth century, Lewis reminds her readers that they have recently been "mere playthings of the imagination, or worse, the mere objects of sensual passion" (43). Now they can be something better. Admitting no inferiority except in terms of physical strength, Lewis describes women as morally superior to men, and she invests their duties with social, political, and religious significance. The success of *Woman's Mission* results from the double-edged nature of its ideology. The terms Lewis helped define—"mission," "sphere," and "influence"—were invoked throughout the period to awaken women's aspirations *and* to curtail their activities.

For Lewis, woman's mission is nothing less than the moral regeneration of mankind in an age marred by "a kind of Epicurean selfishness," a rooted skepticism produced by the materialistic atmosphere and the progress of physical science (127). The Utilitarians had failed to improve society because they emphasized external prosperity and tried to alter social institutions without awakening the individual conscience. Lewis proposes another possibility for social progress, one which can only be undertaken by the mothers of England.

We see, then, how men may be rendered better and happier; in other words, on what principles depends the regeneration of mankind: on the cultivation of the religious and moral portion of their nature, which cultivation no government has yet attempted, over which, in fact, governments and public institutions have little or no control. It is in the cultivation of that divine spirit of unselfish rectitude, which has love for its origin, and the good of others for its aim; a spirit opposed—oh, how opposed—to the selfish and grovelling utilitarianism which it appears to be the unfortunate tendency of physical improvements to promote, and which intellectual culture at best serves but to neutralize. Principles have their chief source in influences; early influences, above all; and early influences have more power in forming character than institutions or mental cultivation; it is therefore to the arbiters of these that we must look for the regenerating principle. We must seek, then, some fundamental principle, some spirit indefatigable, delighting in its task, and which may pervade the whole of society. Such a principle we find in family affection,—especially in maternal affection. Have we, then, been too bold, in asserting that women may be the prime agents of God in the regeneration of mankind? . . .

It is of the utmost consequence to remark, that in children sentiment precedes intelligence; the first answer to the maternal smile is the first dawn of intelligence; the first sensation is the responding caress. Comprehension begins in feeling; hence to her who first arouses the feelings, who first awakens the tenderness, must belong the happiest influences. She is not, however, to teach virtue, but to inspire it. This is peculiarly the province of woman. What she wishes us to be, she begins by making us love, and love begets unconscious imitation. What is a child in relation to a tutor? An ignorant being whom he is called upon to instruct. What is a child in relation to a mother? An immortal being, whose soul it is her business to train for immortality. Good schoolmasters make good scholars,—good mothers make good men; here is the difference of their missions. It follows, that the education, properly so called, of the child, depends almost entirely on mothers. . . . Who better than a mother can teach us to prefer honor to riches—to love our fellow creatures—to raise our souls to the only source of goodness and infinitude. A common tutor counsels and moralizes what he commits to our memory; a mother engraves on our heart; she makes us love what he only makes us believe; it is through love that we arrive at virtue. . . . The political interests, inseparable from the moral interests of mankind, do not depend upon the basis of learning, but of conscience, for their foundation. Learning is only so far valuable as it tends to enlighten and enlarge the views of conscience. Who so fit to lay this foundation as woman, who, to the enlarged capacity of the other sex, should add the uncompromising fidelity, the unselfish devotedness of her own? . . .

Maternal love [is] the only purely unselfish feeling that exists on this earth; the only affection which (as far as it appears,) flows from the loving to the beloved object in one continual stream, uninterrupted by those impediments which check every other. Disease, deformity, ingratitude,—nothing can check the flow of maternal love. By intrusting to woman such a revelation of himself, God has pointed out whom he intends for his missionaries upon earth,—the disseminators of his spirit, the diffusers of his word. Let men enjoy in peace and triumph the intellectual kingdom which is theirs, and which doubtless was intended for them; let us participate its privileges, without desiring to share its dominion. The moral world is ours,—ours by position; ours by qualification; ours by the very indication of God himself. (19-20, 22-24, 129-30)

To exercise her moral power and fulfill her mission, a woman must develop self-renunciation, the source of happiness and "the one quality on which woman's value and influence depend" (50). She also needs the truth of Christianity, "the only scheme which has annexed happiness to self-renunciation, and thus made a revelation of our true and real nature" (135).

It seems to be particularly a part of women's mission to exhibit Christianity in its beauty and purity, and to disseminate it by example and culture. They have the greatest advantage afforded to them for the fulfilment of this mission, and are under the greatest obligations to fulfil it. For woman never would, and never could, have risen to her present station in the social system, had it not been for the dignity with which Christianity invested those qualities peculiarly her own;—no human eye could thus have seen into the deep things of God—no human penetration could have discovered the counsel of Him who has chosen the weak things of this world to confound the strong! No human wisdom could have discovered that pride is not strength, nor self-opinion greatness of soul—nor bravery sublimity—nor glory happiness—and that our highest honor, as creatures, is submission; as sinners, humility; as brethren, love. This revelation at once settled the condition of woman, by exalting her own peculiar qualities in the moral grade. . . .

Let Christianity then be the basis of women's own education—the basis of the education which they give to their children; so shall they perform their mission, not with murmuring and repining at their inferior nature and narrow sphere, but with joy and rejoicing that they are agents in that great work, which, if they are Christians, they daily pray for,—that the kingdom of God may come, and his will be done, as in heaven so on earth. May we have strength and grace to echo this prayer, not only with our lips, but with our lives, and to labor in the cause as those grateful for inestimable benefits, and conscious of their mission. That mission contains, perhaps, the destinies of society: the wish to accomplish it, the means of accomplishing it, should never be out of woman's mind. (142–43, 151–52)

Lewis implores women to accomplish their grand and glorious destiny within the home (See Illustration 1.) By presenting the home as woman's proper sphere, Lewis, like many other writers, is responding to a number of historical conditions: the need for domestic stability in a time of unsettling change; the increased emphasis on early childhood education in post-Enlightenment psychology; and the new methods of production which separated the workplace from the home, taking men to the "time-discipline" of factories and shops while leaving women the "task-oriented" duties of child care and household management.[12] Although Lewis admits that her readers might find a contradiction between the lofty mission and the limited sphere, she maintains that women's salvation is best achieved by the faithful performance of everyday duties.

The fact of moral and intellectual equality being established, it seems somewhat irrational to condemn women to obscurity and detail for their field of exertion, while men usurp the extended one of public usefulness. . . . For it *is* an apparent inconsistency to recommend at the same time expansion of views and contraction of operation; to awaken the sense of power, and to require that the exercise of it be limited; to apply at once the spur and the rein.

1. A Coming Event
Jessica Hayllar, 1886 (*Forbes Magazine Collection*)

2. Home Comforts
Frontispiece to *The Women of England* by Sarah Ellis, n.d.

That intellect is to be invigorated only to enlighten conscience—that conscience is to be enlightened only to act on details—that accomplishments and graces are to be cultivated only, or chiefly, to adorn obscurity;—a list of somewhat paradoxical propositions indeed, and hard to be received. . . .

Those who would be the agents of Providence must observe the workings of Providence, and be content to work also in that way, and by those means, which Almighty wisdom appoints. There is infinite littleness in despising small things. It seems paradoxical to say that there are no small things; our littleness and our aspiration make things appear small. There are, morally speaking, no small duties. Nothing that influences human virtue and happiness can be really trifling, and what more influences them than the despised, because limited, duties assigned to woman? . . . It is true, her reward (her task being done) is not of this world, nor will she wish it to be;—enough for her to be one of the most active and efficient agents in her heavenly Father's work of man's regeneration, enough for her that generations yet unborn shall rise up and call her blessed. (48–49, 67–68)

Lewis acknowledges that some women will be tempted to forsake their sphere, either from an egotistical need to have greater attention, or from "philanthropic Quixotism"—the desire to ameliorate all manner of social distress—but she urges them to remain at home.

And here I would address myself to the educators of female youth, beseeching them to consider the deep importance of their occupation,—entreating them to remember that to them is intrusted the training of beings, whose mission on earth is not only to shine, to please, to adorn, but to influence, and by influencing to regenerate;—that the chief object of their education is not so much to fit them to adorn society, as to vivify and enlighten a home. What a paradise even this world might become, if one half the amount of effort expended in vain attempts to excite the admiration of strangers, were reserved to vary the amusements and adorn the sacred precincts of home! Here is an inexhaustible field of effort, an inexhaustible source of happiness; and here women are the undoubted agents, and they complain of having no scope for exertion! The happiness without which wealth, honors, nay, intellectual pleasures, are but gilded toys, it is theirs to produce and foster; and they have no mission! The only bliss of Paradise that has survived the fall is deposited in their keeping, and they have no importance! . . . Till the philosophy of domestic happiness has undergone a thorough reformation, let not women seek to invade the sphere of the other sex; or we may safely allow those only to do so, who can say with truth that for the comfort, the elegance, the happiness of the home of which they are the tutelary divinities, nothing remains to be done; till home, instead of being a scene of vapid indifference, perhaps of angry contention, is the Elysium of each and all of its sharers,—the favorite field for the exercise of virtues,—the favorite scene of display for graces and accomplishments. (120-22)

Unfortunately the two current systems of female education —"the education of accomplishments for shining in society" and "intellectual education, or that of the mental powers"—do not teach women to appreciate their duties. Because these educational systems encourage self-centeredness and display instead of sacrifice and useful service, Lewis calls for a change.

What then is the true object of female education? The best answer to this question is, a statement of future duties; for it must never be forgotten, that if education be not a training for future duties, it is nothing. The ordinary lot of woman is to marry. Has anything in these educations prepared her to make a wise choice in marriage? To be a mother! Have the duties of maternity,—the nature of moral influence,—been pointed out to her? Has she ever been enlightened as to the consequent unspeakable importance of personal character as the source of influence? In a word, have any means, direct or indirect, prepared her for her duties? No! but she is a linguist, a pianist, graceful, admired. What is that to the purpose? . . . If conscientiousness and unselfishness be the two main supports of women's beneficial influence, how can any education be good which has not the cultivation of these qualities for its first and principal object? The grand objects, then, in the education of women ought to be, the conscience, the heart, and the affections; the development of those moral qualities, which Providence has so liberally bestowed upon them, doubtless with a wise and beneficient purpose. . . .

The issues of such an education will justify the claims made for women in these pages; then the spirit of vanity will yield to the spirit of self-devotion,—that spirit confessedly natural to woman, and only perverted by wrong education. Content with the sphere of usefulness assigned her by nature and nature's God, viewing that sphere with the piercing eye of intellect, and gilding it with the beautiful colors of the imagination, she will cease the vain and almost impious attempt to wander from it. She will see and acknowledge the beauty, the harmony of the arrangement which has made her physical inferiority (the only inferiority which we acknowledge) the very root from which spring her virtues and their attendant influences. (62–63, 65–67)

Sheltered within their sphere, women are free to exercise influence. Like other writers on domesticity, Lewis casts a distrustful glance toward the world beyond the home. Although she asks her readers a question, her language implies the answer: "Would mankind be benefited by the exchange of influence for power in the case of woman? Would the greatest possible good be procured by bringing her out of her present sphere into the arena of public life, by introducing to our homes and to our hearths the violent dissensions, the hard and rancorous feelings, engendered by political strife?" (10–11). Lewis traces the economic competition and political intrigue of public life to the selfishness, the unregulated temper, and the low ambition of the male sex. She does not want to enter their world; nor does she want to exercise power within political institutions. Scorning all talk of equal rights, she explains how women might properly involve themselves in the affairs of the nation.

Because it is perceived that women have a dignity and value greater than society or themselves have discovered; because their talents and virtues place them on a footing of equality with men, it is maintained that their present sphere of action is too contracted a one, and that they ought to share in the public functions of the other sex. Equality, mental and *physical*, is proclaimed! This is matter too ludicrous to be treated anywhere but in a professed satire. . . . Two principal points only can here be brought forward which oppose this plan at the very outset; they are—

1st. Placing the two sexes in the position of rivals, instead of coadjutors, entailing the diminution of female influence.

2nd. Leaving the important duties of woman only in the hands of that part of the sex least able to perform them efficiently.

The principle of divided labor seems to be a maxim of the divine government, as regards the creature. It is only by a concentration of powers to one point that so feeble a being as man can achieve great results. Why should we wish to set aside this salutary law, and disturb the beautiful simplicity of arrangement which has given to man the power, and to woman the influence, to second the plans of Almighty goodness? They are formed to be cooperators, not rivals, in this great work; and rivals they would undoubtedly become if the same career of public ambition, and the same rewards of success were open to both. Woman, at present, is the regulating power of the great social machine, retaining, through the very exclusion complained of, the power to judge of questions by the abstract rules of right and wrong—a power seldom possessed by those whose spirits are chafed by opposition, and heated by personal contest.

The second resulting evil is a grave one, though in treating of it, also, it is difficult to steer clear of ludicrous associations. The political career being open to women, it is natural to suppose that all the most gifted of the sex would press forward to confer upon their country the benefit of their services, and to reap for themselves the distinction which such services would obtain; the duties hitherto considered peculiar to the sex would sink to a still lower position in public estimation than they now hold, and would be abandoned to those least able conscientiously to fulfil them. The combination of legislative and maternal duties would indeed be a difficult task, and, of course, the least ostentatious would be sacrificed. . . .

How then are women to interfere in politics? As moral agents; as representatives of the moral principle; as champions of the right in preference to the expedient; by their endeavors to instil into their relatives of the other sex the uncompromising sense of duty and self-devotion, which ought to be *their* ruling principles! . . . It is by no means affirmed, that women's political feelings are always guided by the abstract principles of right and wrong; but they are surely more likely to be so, if they themselves are restrained from the public expression of them. . . . It is of the utmost importance to men to feel, in consulting a wife, a mother, or a sister, that they are appealing *from* their passions and prejudices, and not *to* them as embodied in a second self: nothing tends to give opinions such weight as the certainty, that the utterer of them is free from all petty or personal motives. The beneficial influence of woman is nullified if once her motives, or her personal character, come to be the subject of attack; and this fact alone ought to induce her patiently to acquiesce in the plan of seclusion from public affairs. . . .

Removed from the actual collision of political contests, and screened from the passions which such engender, she brings party questions to the test of the unalterable principles of reason and religion; she is, so to speak, the guardian angel of man's political integrity, liable at the best to be warped by passion or prejudice, and excited by the rude clashing of opinions and interests. This is the true secret of woman's political influence, the true object of her political enlightenment. Governments will never be perfect till all distinction between private and public virtue, private and public honor, be done away! Who so fit an agent for the operation of this change as enlightened, unselfish woman? Who so fit, in her two-fold capacity of companion and early instructor, to teach men to prefer honor to gain, duty to ease, public to private interests, and God's work to man's inventions? And shall it be said that women have no political existence, no political influence, when the very germs of political regeneration may spring from them alone, when the fate of nations yet unborn may depend upon the use which they make of the mighty influences committed to their care? The blindness which sees not how these influences would be lessened by taking her out of the sphere assigned by Providence, if voluntary, is wicked,—if real, is pitiable. As well might we desire the earth's beautiful satellite to give place to a second sun, thereby producing the intolerable and glaring continuity of perpetual day. (44-46, 52-53, 66-67)

Periodicals representing a range of opinions on the Woman Question gave enthusiastic reviews to *Woman's Mission*. In America *Godey's* recommended the text to "every woman who wishes to understand her *duties* as well as her rights." The 1839 *Athenaeum* noted that *Woman's Mission* was "strongly marked by the best characteristics of female mind,—large sympathies, abiding affections, logic of the heart rather than of the understanding, the power of persuading rather than convincing." The 1841 *Edinburgh Review*, which declared that women's minds were innately inferior to men's and that proposals to reform their schools were pointless, commended Lewis' little book for "much good sense and good feeling well-expressed." At the other end of the spectrum, the *Westminister Review*, an early supporter of women's equality, spoke highly of the "deservedly popular work." While disagreeing with Lewis' ideas about education, the reviewer conceded that in 1841 no one "has done more to improve and modernize the common notions of female duty than the author of 'Woman's Mission.'"[13] Even Marion Reid, Lewis' most stringent critic, agreed that she had "escaped in a great measure from the thraldom of old prejudices with regard to women."[14]

There were, however, practical and theoretical objections to the book. Lewis' vision did not reflect the realities of life in an industrialized society. Studying the conditions in factories and mines for an 1843 *Athenaeum* series, critic Anna Jameson observed that women forced into such exhausting and degrading work could not fulfill an exalted mission at home. "'Woman's mission,' of which people talk so well and write so prettily, is irreconcilable with woman's position, of which no one dares to think, much less to speak."[15] On a philosophical level, the 1840 *West-*

minister Review took issue with Lewis' ethics: by treating virtue as a female attribute, Lewis implied that men did not need to develop moral responsibility; by basing her argument for women's improvement on their obligation to serve their families, she denied their autonomy.[16]

The most sustained analysis of *Woman's Mission* came in 1843 when Marion Reid wrote *A Plea for Woman*.[17] In 1840 Reid had attended the World's Anti-Slavery Convention in London. She must have seen Lucretia Mott, Lydia Child, and other women in the American delegation censured by the British clergy and denied their seats. Seated with Amelia Opie and Anna Jameson, she probably heard the Rev. George Harvey declaim:

> It is a matter of conscience with me. . . . I have certain views in relation to the teaching of the Word of God, and of the particular sphere in which woman is to act. . . . If I were to give a vote in favor of females, sitting and deliberating in such an assembly as this, I should be acting in opposition to the plain teaching of the Word of God.[18]

Three years later, Reid became alarmed by the wide circulation of Lewis' tract. She published *A Plea for Woman* to show

> . . . that social equality with man is necessary for the free growth and development of woman's nature; that it could not elevate her to complete equality with man, if she be really inferior to him in physical strength and mental vigour; that there is no good ground for the assumption that the possession and exercise of political privileges are incompatible with the right performance of the home duties of the sex; that this equality belongs of right to woman, as possessed of the same rational and responsible nature as man; and that it would be of benefit also to man, by ennobling the influence over him of that being who is the natural companion of his life. (xxvii)

In arguing for equal rights, Reid maintains the centrality of marriage: she claims that educated and active women will make better wives and that their involvement in public affairs will not interfere with home duties. Domestic tranquility will remain undisturbed; in case of a political disagreement at home, the woman would invariably give way, preferring to "suffer a wrong than inflict one" (76). Although the most radical writers regard the family as a cause of women's oppression, Reid speaks for the great majority of nineteenth-century feminists who use the importance of domestic responsibilities as a way of demonstrating the wide range of women's abilities and as an argument for granting them political and educational rights.

Moreover, she insists that woman must achieve independence in order to be a true helpmate to man, and in the best Protestant tradition, she vows that obedience is ultimately owed to a higher authority than a husband. The noble duty of self-renunciation can easily become "a most criminal self-extinction," she writes. "Although in one sense woman was made for man, yet in another and higher she was also made for herself. The more faithful she is to the higher end of her being, the development of her whole nature, moral and rational, the better will she fulfill the lower one, of ministering to the happiness of man" (47). Defending women's right to self-development, Reid produces a searching criticism of Lewis' philosophy, rejecting "influence," extending "sphere," and redefining "mission."

> . . . We are both willing and happy to believe that the influence of woman procures for her a great deal of tenderness, consideration, and courtesy; but this is true only in individual cases. The personal influence of a woman with her husband, and his kindness and good sense, prevent many a woman from having the least suspicion of the barbarous nature of those laws which would interpose but slight obstacles to her husband's treating her with the most unrelenting tyranny, did this mutual good understanding fail. . . . Although, then, there may be thousands of women whose personal influence has prevented them from ever experiencing any very harsh or unjust treatment,—yet, for the whole *sex*, this so-much-talked-of influence has utterly failed in obtaining even the faintest semblance of justice. . . .
>
> The writer of "Woman's Mission" has insisted very much on the conceit—for we can call it nothing else—of giving power to man, and influence to woman. Now, we can see no reason whatever for this division. We think that the theory, that power destroys influence, instead of strengthening and confirming it, is built on a foundation of sand. The partition of power and influence between man and woman certainly does not at present exist—for man now exercises at least as much influence as woman, and has all his power and privileges to add authority to that influence. The common sense and justice of the matter seems to us to be—let every one have equality of right or power, and let our own character give us all the influence it can. . . .

We have still to add a few words to those of our readers who may approve of women taking an interest in politics, but who may think at the same time, that female influence is a very good substitute for the more direct and straight-forward course of allowing them to express their opinions by voting. We think, that as a substitute for the open and direct method, female influence is a mere phantasm: either it means nothing at all, else it has a bad meaning. It resolves itself into the same kind of influence as is exerted by clear reason and strong argument, whether produced by a man or a woman—whether spoken or written; or else it is an instrument which no conscientious woman could justify herself in the use of. If a lady, by force of reason alone, brings a gentleman round to her view of any question, it is an abuse of the term, to say that this is accomplished by female influence: it is an influence which might as well have been employed by another man—by the still colder means of a book even, or by the more careful consideration of the subject by the gentleman himself. If, however, failing to convince his understanding, she succeeds in subduing it to her will by female arts and blandishments, this would, indeed, be the triumph of female influence, but such a triumph as no honourable woman would ever avail herself of. . . .

Having thus, as briefly as possible, pointed out to our readers the most prevalent errors with regard to woman's influence, we proceed to call their attention to some other opinions, equally fallacious, with regard to the nature and extent of woman's sphere. . . . There is at present, we believe, almost every variety of sentiment on this subject, from the narrowest and most bigoted to the most extended and liberal; but we think that the three following classes of opinions will be found, without much straining, to comprehend them all.

1st. Those who think that woman's sphere really and truly comprises only her domestic duties, and that her mind ought never to stir beyond these.

2d. Those who think her mind ought to be enlarged, and her condition improved in some respects; but that she ought not to be equally privileged with man.

3d. Those who think she has a just claim to equal rights with man.

These fears of confusion and disorder in society, were the circumstance of sex alone not allowed to operate as a disqualification for any privilege, appear to take two directions. The first, that it would occasion a hostile collision between the sexes; the other, that the household virtues, and domestic duties and pleasures of woman, would alike be neglected and spurned for what we may call more ambitious pursuits. But are fears, in either of these directions, at all compatible with the idea, much less with a sincere and hearty belief in the idea, that the sexes are marked by nature with many distinctions, both physical and mental, fitting them for different spheres of action which have been appointed them by Providence? . . .

There is yet another consideration connected with this subject, worthy of our attention. If all woman's duties are to be considered as so strictly domestic, and if God and nature have really so circumscribed her sphere of action—what are we to think of the dreadful depravity of thousands upon thousands of unprotected females, who actually prefer leaving their only proper sphere, and working for their own subsistence—to starvation? Is it not shocking to see their consciences so seared, that they are quite unaware of the dreadful nature of the course they are following? Ought not such wicked creatures to be exterminated? Or if we charitably allow them to cover their sins under the strong plea of necessity, what are we to think of that state of society which absolutely forces thousands of unfortunates to contradict their own nature—not by enlightening or enlarging their sphere—but by thrusting them entirely out of it? . . .

If we cannot, by any regulations, prevent the necessity which induces so many women to devote themselves to labour for themselves and those who are dear to them—if we do not even wish to prevent this necessity, but rather, on the contrary, to provide greater facilities for female exertion—is it fair to keep up the distinctions in the opposite quarter? If the necessities of our social system force one part of the sex to leave the domestic sphere entirely, to work at some trade or business, surely it is a mere pretence to make the conservation of this peculiar sphere an excuse for hindering some others of the sex from leaving it, in the very slight degree which is necessary to enable them to exercise all the privileges we seek for them. . . .

We ourselves hold, we hope with many more, that woman has a right to social equality; and we also maintain, that the possession of this just right would not interfere in the slightest with her domestic duties, or "woman's sphere," as it is called. Nay, we go still farther, and assert, that the energy, self-reliance, and intelligence, which the possession of this right has such a tendency to foster and call into action, would be highly favourable to a more enlarged view of those duties and a more active discharge of them. . . .

Of course, no one wishes to take her out of what he considers her true and proper sphere. We should think there could not be two opinions as to the propriety of her moving in the sphere which God and nature intended her to fill; the only difficulty is in deciding what that true and natural sphere is. As long as opinions are so various on that point, it is not very philosophical to use the phrase as if its meaning were quite undisputed. . . .

In taking a general review of our subject, the idea that strikes us most forcibly is, that the grand objection to our opinions—that they are calculated to overturn the natural order of things—proceeds entirely from a want of faith in that very nature which yet has the semblance of being an object of the firmest trust. . . . If, then, nature has made so many distinctions between the sexes, and consequently between their spheres of action, as is generally believed, ought it to be credited that the mere removal of one or two human restraints will have the effect of destroying those with which nature herself has surrounded woman? No. . . . Those who fear such a result, show, by that very fear, how feeble is their assurance that the sphere, to which they would have woman confined, is really the only sphere appointed her by Providence. The providence of God has set bounds to the sea; does man, then, find it necessary to give his feeble aid of dikes and ramparts to assist this provision of nature? Or, is it not rather when he drives back the ocean, and takes possession of its bed, that these dikes and ramparts become necessary to restrain the mighty deep? Nay, were every such bulwark of man against the ocean destroyed in an instant, would even the strong reaction against restraint enable it to advance beyond its natural limits? As surely, although woman were a free as the winds, she will never go beyond the sphere appointed her by Providence.

Again we would repeat, that though no scheme would be of a healthy complexion, the object or the consequence of which was to take woman away from domestic occupations, (or in other words, make woman change places with man, for one of them must attend to these matters,) so neither is there justice, to either sex, in the social system which tries to confine them to those occupations. We say tries, for it only succeeds in throwing obstacles in the way of woman's sphere being enlarged judiciously, and in a right direction. We hope, then, that we have made it sufficiently clear to our readers, that the use of the phrase "woman's sphere," in the manner in which it generally is employed, is a mere gratuitous assumption by the writer who employs it, that his idea of the extent of woman's duties is the correct one. (7–10, 154–55, 12–16, 144–46, 22, 153–154, 24)

Marion Reid argues that women should be allowed to vote as well as to work. For her, politics is synonymous with "patriotism and philanthropy," and the deprivation of equal civil rights is "the fertile source of many other evils, as well as the most injurious in itself."

The exercise of those rights would be useful in two ways: it would tend to ennoble and elevate the mind; and it would secure the temporal interest of those who exercise it. . . . The consciousness of a responsibility which the possession of a vote would bestow, the dignity of being trusted, the resolution to justify the faith placed in her truth and judgment, would call forth, in woman, noble powers, which, hitherto, have been too much suffered to lie dormant. . . .

But besides all this, equal privileges are necessary for the mere temporal interests of all; for no one can be supposed to know so well as the individual himself, what is for his own peculiar advantage. . . . [The laws] are in themselves a convincing proof, first, that woman requires representation, and second, that she is not represented. So utterly unjust are they—as we shall show when treating more particularly on that subject,—that no real representative of woman could have any share in the making of them. . . .

Every woman—and every man, too—has, indeed a mission and a noble one, in the world; but in vain shall we look for zealous missionaries in those whose minds are reduced to such a wretchedly-degraded level as to be stupidly insensible to the insult of having their whole sex classed with children, malefactors, and the miserable victims of mental imbecility. . . . As long as woman reposes with indolent security on the reason of man, and refuses to exert her own, her mission in the world will have but little success. She must be fully enfranchised before she can either see clearly the scope of her mission, or be sufficiently aroused to engage in it. The first step in the process is to show her her shackled condition. At present, alas! she cannot even wish and strive for freedom!—she knows not that she is in any need of it. She is poor and miserable, blind and naked; and by imagining that she is quite the reverse, loses the power she could otherwise exert of trying to improve her condition.

There are some few who have been awakened from this pleasing but ignoble dream, whose blood boils and thrills with indignant feeling at finding themselves so classed; but they are so few that, as a party, they have no name. By too many, they and their opinions, are regarded with derision and contempt. Without putting themselves to the trouble of examining into the right or the wrong of the matter, most people smile disdainfully when the rights of woman are mentioned. Still, let not the enlightened among women be discouraged. Let me implore them to allow "the world's dread laugh" to pass by them as the idle wind which they regard not. . . . Let them look back to the time, not very far distant, when the slavery of the whole negro race was justified as an institution of divine origin; and, when they notice the great change which has taken place in public opinion since those days, let them not despair of an equally great, or an equally speedy change in those matters in which they are so deeply interested. (36–39, 63–65)

For women, as for blacks, such optimism was unwarranted.[19] The campaign for female enfranchisement, which Reid saw as a way to exercise political power rather than personal influence, did not succeed until the second decade of the twentieth century. In trying to dismiss the doctrine of woman's sphere because it had "no definite, precise, and unmistakable meaning" (20), Reid was also ahead of her time. Only the most radical feminists— Thompson, Martineau, Taylor, Mill—believed that the philosophy was a coercive social construct which must be entirely set aside. More typically and more successfully, Victorian feminists used the doctrine of the spheres to gain specific reforms, especially in the area of education.[20] While opponents of women's rights continued throughout the period to cite circumscribed versions of woman's sphere in their arguments against equality in work, education, and politics, many feminists accepted, and indeed acted upon, the spiritual and moral qualities Lewis attributed to them. By 1858 the *Saturday Review* had perceived the danger.

> There is a little too much of a "woman's mission" style of writing. Of course it is right to hold out a high standard, and, of course, women have a mission, if by a mission is meant that they have duties to perform, and that there is every reason to suppose they were called into existence for some wise purpose. But the expression "woman's mission" is meant to do more than convey this. It is meant to create, by its vast grandiloquence, the notion that women have something sublime and mysterious to do which, until lately, no one ever heard.[21]

Apocalyptic feminism—the claim for women's superiority— simply carried Lewis' argument to its extreme.

2

William Thompson and Appeal of One Half the Human Race

William Thompson, the forgotten man of the woman's movement, wrote in 1825 the most important feminist work between Mary Wollstonecraft's *Vindication of the Rights of Woman* (1792) and the High Victorian masterpieces of George Drysdale (II,2) and J.S. Mill. *Appeal of One Half the Human Race*[1] is particularly powerful because Thompson articulates a comprehensive philosophy based upon theoretical and practical economics. He goes beyond specific grievances to the basic causes of human misery. Seeking, like many of his contemporaries, to effect human happiness by creating a "social science" which would affect the organization of society, Thompson espouses women as part of his espousal of all victims of society. In the process Thompson anticipates virtually every issue of the Woman Question (and these books)—the equation of women with children and with blacks, the relevance of physical size and brain weight to equality, the role of work, the moral efficacy of capitalism and competition, the nature of woman's sexuality, the right of women to preach, even male attraction to sickness.

Thompson begins his career by practicing what he will later preach. In 1814 he takes over the family's Irish estate in Glenore. Its eight hundred acres boast seven hundred beggars. Dividing the land into tenant farms, Thompson teaches the new theory of spade cultivation, founds a school to teach children the latest agricultural methods, and lays out a model farm. By 1834 "fifty seven [tenants] had 'paid their rent every farthing'; the remaining three had only failed 'in consequence of some family misfortune.'"[2] An eccentric beloved of the people, Thompson wars against everything from Demon Rum to Holy Church, including physicians, lawyers, and absentee landlords..

Thompson's commitment to social reform drives him into public affairs in 1818. Appalled at the mismanagement of the Cork Institute, Thompson moves characteristically from specific grievances to general principles—from misspent funds to the nature of education.

> [The school should aim] not to make linguists, or mathematicians, or astronomers, or antiquarian dilettanti, but to make useful citizens for active life, to make intelligent and respectable, and benevolent tradesmen and merchants and country gentlemen, and to make their wives and daughters equally intelligent, respectable and useful.[3]

Educational reform is one of the several passions which Thompson shares with Jeremy Bentham, whom he visits in 1822—beginning what is intellectually the most important time of Thompson's life. He had been reading many of the major thinkers for years and had already visited Paris, but it is through Bentham that Thompson at last meets the leading Utilitarians and encounters firsthand the dominant ideas of Britain and the Continent. In this intellectually challenging environment Thompson writes what is to he his masterpiece, *Inquiry into the Principles of the Distribution of Wealth* (1824). No sooner is this book received enthusiastically by the Utilitarians than Thompson runs head-on into one of Utilitarianism's chief spokesmen, James Mill. Mill in 1825 reprints in pamphlet form his "Article on Government," which maintained

> One thing is pretty clear, that all those individuals whose interests are indisputably included in those of other individuals may be struck off from political rights without inconvenience. In this light may be viewed all children up to a certain age, whose interests are

involved in those of their parents. In this light also women may be regarded, the interest of almost all of whom is involved either in that of their fathers, or in that of their husbands.[4]

William Thompson replies with *Appeal of One Half the Human Race*.

I

In the *Appeal* Thompson demonstrates his knowledge of previous feminist writers. Although he speaks respectfully of "that neglected banner which a woman's hand nearly thirty years ago unfolded boldly, in the face of the prejudices of thousands of years," Thompson also notes "the narrow views which too often marred Mary Wollstonecraft's pages and narrowed their usefulness" and "the timidity and impotence of conclusion accompanying the gentle eloquence of Mary Hays" (vii). To understand Thompson's own contribution, we must understand his tie to four persons and several ideas.

Startling—then and now—is the fact that the "Article on Government" was written, not by a "reactionary," but by a "radical." Utilitarians generally favored women's rights. Thompson reacts strongly to Mill's "Article" partly because he feels that the radical cause has been betrayed from within. Although he acknowledges with typical fairness that James Mill achieved much for *men* in the "Article" and that Mill had at least forsaken most of the most egregious arguments against women, Thompson contends that "the latest and most enlightened system of philosophy, the glorious principle of Utility itself, hardly born, is prostituted" (195). Especially since Bentham and many established Utilitarians had remonstrated with James Mill, and since J.S. Mill and the younger radicals "most positively dissented,"[5] Thompson wants unequivocally to separate Mill's chauvinism from Bentham's cause.

> Thus cavalierly are dealt with by this philosopher of humanity, the interests of one half the human species! Not so Mr. Bentham, whose disciple he is: the philosophy of that enlightened and benevolent man, embraces in its grasp every sentient human being, and acknowledges the claim of every rational adult, without distinction of sex or colour, to equal political rights. Is the authority of the disciple above that of the master? (9–10)

The ideas which Thompson defends so ardently are the key-stones of "liberal" economics. He basically combines Bentham and Robert Owen—the doctrine of Utility (the greatest happiness for the greatest number) and a belief in Collectivism (mankind can respond to incentives other than love of riches or fear of starvation). Agreeing with Sismondi and Saint-Simon that competition causes intolerable social evils, and accepting Ricardo's thesis that the value of an article is determined by the amount of labor required to produce it, Thompson believes that woman cannot be fully happy until she gets back from her labor all that she has put into it. Only when Collectivism replaces Competition will the greatest number of citizens achieve the greatest possible happiness.

Besides James Mill and Bentham, two other persons important to Thompson are Anna Wheeler and J.S. Mill. Mentioning Wheeler and J.S. Mill together is appropriate because Mill's famous tribute to Harriet Taylor in the dedication to *On Liberty* resembles strikingly Thompson's earlier homage to Anna Wheeler in the *Appeal*.

> I have endeavored to arrange the expression of those feelings, sentiments, and reasonings, which have emanated from your mind. In the following pages you will find discussed on paper, what you have so often discussed in conversation. . . . To separate your thoughts from mine were now to me impossible, so amalgamated are they with my own. . . . (v,vi)
>
> *To the beloved and deplored memory of her who was the inspirer, and in part the author, of all that is best in my writings. . . . this volume . . . belongs as much to her as to me. (On Liberty)*[6]

Anna Wheeler, intelligent, beautiful, erudite, charming, and disastrously wed, knows all the leading radicals of Europe (including Fourier in Paris before he was famous). She writes for cooperative periodicals and does what then, and for the next half century, is most forward: she lectures publicly. So enthusiastic is she for the French Revolution of 1830 that partisans send her a knot of tricolor taken from the barricades. Meeting William Thompson in 1824, Wheeler finds a man of energetic brilliance who shares her ideas and ideals. She discusses with him the sufferings inflicted upon women by the economic system and by rigid institutions and conventions; with him she rages at James Mill's "Article" (and at its dismissing woman in only seven lines!). Corroborating Thompson's deeply felt admission of Wheeler's influence is the touching testimony of a Dutch contemporary: "On opening Thompson's old book the nobility of Anna Wheeler's figure and the sweetness of her expression stand out like a pressed flower discovered anew."[7]

J.S. Mill shares with Thompson more than an indebtedness to strong-minded women. Having "most positively dissented" from his father's position on woman, the younger Mill is inevitably open to Thompson's arguments. In the year of the *Appeal*, Thompson helps found the Cooperative debates which J.S. Mill and his newly formed Utilitarian Society attend. Forty years later Mill recalled in his *Autobiography* that

> The principal champion of their [the Owenite] side was a very estimable man, with whom I was well acquainted, Mr. William Thompson, of Cork, author of a book on the Distribution of Wealth, and of an "Appeal" in behalf of women against the passage relating to them in my father's Essay on Government.[8]

Thompson's influence lasts as long as his memory. Not only does the older man's critique of laissez-faire affect the younger's economic thought, but Mill's *Subjection* resembles Thompson's *Appeal* in ways too important to be accidental. Both men examine the notion and nature of the "contract" in marriage; both emphasize the despotic power of husbands; both place special emphasis upon the intellectual and spiritual equality of the sexes, and argue that only such equality can free wife *and* husband from the slavery of her servitude.

II

In James Mill's argument from common conjugal interest, Thompson is confronting one of the most formidable assumptions of the culture. Forty years before, the framers of the American Constitution had used common interest to justify excluding wives from the franchise; forty years after Thompson's *Appeal*, the Mrs. Ellises and Mrs. Lintons of High Victorian orthodoxy define as one prerequisite of the wifely ideal a woman's willingness to equate her interests and her husband's; in 1881, so emancipated a young American as Isabel Archer will say of her domineering husband in Henry James's *The Portrait of a Lady*, "he had expected his wife to feel with him and for him, to enter into his opinions, his ambitions, his preferences; and Isabel was obliged to confess that this was no very unwarrantable demand on the part of a husband."[9] In fact, the argument from common conjugal interest endures in various forms well into the twentieth century.

So deeply rooted an attitude is not easy for Thompson to discredit. He attacks James Mill's "Article" on two fronts—first, the "general argument," then its application to women. In Mill's general argument Thompson finds a contradiction between how men treat the whole human race and how they supposedly treat half of that race, women.

> Were Mr. Mill's system of philosophy founded on the assumption that *man* was naturally and necessarily a beneficent being, always inclined to promote the happiness of those within his power, and necessarily acquainted with the means to promote this end in a degree superior to that possessed by those over whom his power extended; however fond and puerile we might conceive the assumption, the *inference*, that power over others might be safely placed in his hands, would be at least fairly drawn from the premises.
>
> But, strange to say, the assumption, on which the whole fabric of Mr. Mill's philosophy rests, is directly opposed to any such notion of natural beneficence and unerring judgment on the part of men. Mr. Mill's philosophical basis of reasoning is, that *all* men are necessarily inclined to use for their own exclusive advantage whatever power they can acquire over the actions of their fellowmen, and that the more knowledge they happen to possess, with the more skill will they use this power to promote such exclusive interest, at the expense of those over whom their power extends. . . .
>
> Still, however, in the face of this grand governing law of human nature, this male philosopher maintains, that, with respect to *one half* the human race, women, this universal disposition of man to use power for his own exclusive benefit ceases, and his knowledge with respect to them, invariably shows him that their happiness coincides with his, and is included in it! This exception of one half from the influence of the general rule of the disposition to misuse power, is certainly a pretty large exception, requiring all the boldness of an English philosopher. In any other hands, so large an exception would go far to destroy the rule. An exception of one half! . . .

But the truth is, that all such quibbling and vain distinctions are unworthy the name of philosophy. Men without knowledge or benevolence, or placed in such circumstances as are ordinarily incompatible with the exercise of such qualities, will necessarily use power for their own apparent exclusive benefit, at the expense of all other sentient beings, children, women, or other men, whose interests may *appear* to them incompatible with their own. Nor is there any mysterious identification or inclusion of the interests of the weak and ignorant with those of the strong and knowing. On the contrary, the more ignorant and the more weak . . . the less will there be, or appear to be, of identification or inclusion of interests. . . .

From this examination it results, that the pretext set up to exclude women from political rights, namely, the inclination of men to use power over them beneficently, would, if admitted, sweep away the grand argument itself for the political rights of men; inasmuch as it would prove men to be inclined to use power, though without limits or checks, *beneficently*, over at least half their race. Whence the argument founded on the contrary supposition, that of the universal love of power for *selfish* purposes, must fall. The penalty of injustice, to women is, therefore, the justification, by the most simple and unanswerable reasoning, of similar injustice from men to men. (4–5, 7, 12, 19)

Turning to Mill's particular argument about women, Thompson asks three questions. I: Do men and women, in fact, share basic interests in common? II: Which sex, if either, should be denied civil and political rights? III: Can equality of enjoyments be secured without civil and political equality? To answer Question I, Thompson seizes immediately upon Mill's phrase "almost all women":

The first obvious defect in Mr. Mill's position, the basis of his system of *universal* exclusion against women, must strike every eye. . . . "*Almost* all women [says Mill] find their interests involved either in that of their fathers or in that of their husbands: therefore *all* women should be excluded from political rights." (28)

If women with fathers or husbands need no political rights, then women without fathers or husbands do need such rights. Spinsters, widows, adult women living away from home: "How large a portion of the adults of the human race do the above three classes form! from one sixth to perhaps one fourth" (31). After demonstrating that daughters share with fathers only one interest—to be married off as soon as possible—Thompson focuses upon marriage and thus upon Mill's main point. Do wives, in fact, share basic interests with their husbands? Thompson, like Marion Reid later [I.1], calls seriously into question the nature and extent of woman's private influence.

We have already seen, in the case of adult daughters, that the law itself disallows the pretext of an identity of interest between daughters and fathers, by taking away from the father all *direct* control over the actions of daughters to the same extent as over those of sons. From the time of adolescence up to the time of marriage, the law of England supposes a perfect capacity on the part of the adult woman as well as of the adult man. . . . But as soon as adult daughters become wives, their civil rights disappear; they fall back again, and remain all their lives—should their owners and directors live so long—into the state of children or idiots, the passive property of their owners; protected by the law in some few respects only, like other slaves, from the excessive abuse of despotic power. What is this mysterious circumstance in the connexion of marriage, which alters so completely the nature and interests of woman as an individual, rational, and sentient being. . . . In marriage, it will perhaps be said—for we are really anxious to penetrate the remotest, most delicate, things approaching to reasons on so mysterious a subject—man becomes dependent for one of the most copious sources of his happiness, that arising from sexual endearments, on his wife, and is therefore compelled to a kindly use of whatever despotic powers law may give him, in order to procure from woman those gratifications, the zest of which depends on the kindly inclinations of the party yielding them.

Were women utterly destitute of those feelings which render men dependent on them for their gratification; were sensibility no part of their organization, instead of being, as it now is, preposterously over-excited; were they cold as stones to feeling and to love; or had they self-control and magnanimity enough to obey the invitation of the celebrated Grecian, Aspasia, to repress their own feelings, and make their power of gratifying the imperious propensities of men, their masters, subservient to the acquiring of an equality of rights and enjoyments with their masters;—then, and in either of these cases, would there be some force in the observation, that the dependence of man for sexual enjoyment on woman necessitated a kindly use of the despotic power he usurped over her when living with her for the rearing of a family. But such is not the constitution of the human frame, such is not the constitution of woman; such is not her power of command over her feelings; such is not her comprehensiveness of mind, stunted by disuse and want of education. *Woman is more the slave of man for the gratification of her desires, than man is of woman.* To man, unmarried and speculating on marriage, by the permission of law and of public opinion, the gratification of every sexual desire is permitted, limited only by prudential considerations as to money and health, and with some few by considerations as to the effects of their actions on the happiness of those connected with them; while to woman speculating on marriage . . . the gratification to her of these same desires is altogether prohibited. To man married, for breach of the vain and insulting promise of fidelity to his wife, no penalty is awarded by law; while public opinion extenuates the venial offence, or rather encourages and smiles upon it: while to woman married, the breach of the compulsory vow of slavish obedience, is punished at command of the husband, even by aid of the civil power; and the vow of fidelity—no empty vow to her—is enforced by the united ruin and degradation of law and public opinion, both created by man for his exclusive benefit, and unrelentingly enforced.

But this is not all. Woman can demand no enjoyment from man as a matter of right: she must beg it, like any of her children, or like any slave, as a favor. If refused, she must submit, contented or not contented. Once married, a woman must submit to the *commands* of her master. Superstition is called in to the aid of despotism, and at the altar woman is constrained to devote herself a victim to the gratification of all the pleasures and legal commands (extending to all actions not erected by the law into crimes) of her owner, renouncing the voluntary direction of her own actions in favor of the man who has admitted her to the high honor of becoming his involuntary breeding machine and household slave. What then becomes of the pretended dependence of man on the voluntary compliance of woman in marriage with any of his inclinations? . . . Man disdains to beg for what he can command. . . . Not only does woman obey; the despotism of man demands another sacrifice. Woman must cast nature, or feign to cast it, from her breast. She is not permitted to appear to feel, or desire. The whole of what is called her education training her to be the obedient instrument of man's sensual gratification, she is not permitted even to wish for any gratification for herself. She must have no desires: she must always yield, must submit as a matter of duty, not repose upon her equal for the sake of happiness: she must blush to own that she joys in his generous caresses, were such by chance ever given. This engrafted duplicity of character still further increases, and to an incalculable extent, the dependence of woman in marriage on man; his slave for what nature has implanted as the most innocent and useful of human desires, when not gratified at the expense of ulterior mischief or of any fellow-creature's happiness; doubly his slave, from the necessity of concealing these natural desires, and from the heartless insult with which the brutal male sensualist is wont to repress the gentlest, the humblest, the most kindly overflowings of them. . . .

If the disposition to promote the happiness of another to an equal degree with our own exist, and the same power be applicable to both, the happiness of both will be in point of fact equally promoted. Happiness is the aggregate; of which pleasures are the items. Do wives enjoy as many pleasures of all sorts as their husbands, having the guardianship of their volitions, do? This is the experimental touchstone to prove or disprove an identity of interest, or an involving, as it is called, of the happiness of one human being in that of another. Let us go through the different pleasures of which rational sentient beings are susceptible. First, of the senses and internal excitement. . . . The same indulgence in sensual pleasures which is freely permitted to himself and his associates, is held quite unseemly in his weaker companion. Eating or drinking to excess, either in quantity or quality of food, which is regarded by many as the prerogative of man rich enough to enjoy them, or to be limited only by a prudential regard to immediate health, is looked upon as disgusting in woman. . . . The [sensual] happiness of wives is not involved in that of their husbands, is not promoted to the same extent as their own. . . .

From intellectual, from social or sympathetic pleasures, which so elevate the human race in the scale of being and capability of happiness over all other animals . . . which occupy so great a space of time and human life with gentle and never over-exciting emotion, which are so cheap of purchase, requiring nothing but culture for their enjoyment, women, and particularly wives, are brutally excluded, with the real but vain object of adding to man's voluptuous enjoyments, and of pampering his conceit of superiority and his unhallowed love of despotic command. From want of education, of early culture, *equal to that of men*, in every branch of useful knowledge, women lose the immense accession to their happiness which intellectual culture would afford them. From hours and nights and days of interesting conversation, they are excluded: to silence or retirement they are driven, while the males are glowing with interest, enjoying the emotions of curiosity, judgment, anticipation. Besides the total loss to women, how much would man's enjoyment of these pleasures be increased, by doubling the number of persons capable of sharing them with him, and of associating them with so many other pleasures! From the seclusion from events and knowledge in which women are brought up, and from the ignorance which is thus forced upon them, the herd of men unavoidably contract an habitual contempt for their intellectual powers, and repress as presumption an opinion, even timidly given by them, on any subject beyond the grasp of children's minds.

If from intellectual pleasures we turn to those of sympathy, or of the social class, we shall find a contrast almost as marked and barefaced between the enjoyments of the two parties, husbands and wives. . . . Is there a wife who dares to form her own acquaintances amongst women or men, without the permission, direct or indirect, of the husband to form such acquaintances, or to retain them when formed? Is there a husband who would not spurn the permission, direct or implied, of the wife to form or retain such acquaintances? . . . From friendship, if we proceed to attachments, persecution desolation and death attend the footsteps of the wife if the husband only *suspect* them, (for permission or even connivance is not only here out of the question, but to look for it would be deemed insanity on the part of the wife, and to grant it would be deemed on the part of the husband degradation and immorality,) though his own attachments were as extensive and public as those of any Eastern despot. Is there, on the contrary, any husband who would not conceive his right of sovereignty, his power to make wretched, the badge of his manhood, compromised, by permitting his wife to pry into or interfere with his attachments or connexions amongst men or women? Cut off and isolated from all human society and social endearment is the wife, except in as far as the husband permits. . . .

[T]he civilized wife is liable to the uncontrolled and eternal caprices of an ever-jealous and ever-present tyrant: a tyrant, beneficent *if he pleases*, but still a tyrant because he retains the uncontrolled *power* of being wicked, of making his fellow-creature wretched, at his pleasure. Till laws afford married women the same protection against the restraints and violence of . . . their husbands, that their husbands enjoy against their caprices and violence, the social condition of the civilized wife will remain more completely slavish than that of the female slave of the West Indies; and triumphantly will remain established, here amongst us, without traveling to the East or the West in pursuit of it, the truth of Mr. Mill's position, that "men possessing power without checks will necessarily use it at the expense of others till they reduce them to the state, at least, of the slaves in the West Indies." (58–64; 76, 78, 80, 82, 84–85, 88–89)

To Question II—which sex, if either, should be deprived of civil and political rights—Thompson's answer is expectable. Both should be equal, but deprivation, if unavoidable, should befall men. Woman's capacity for sympathy is the chief requisite for a legislator, more important than the male traits of expertise and "genius"; woman's physical inferiority would prevent her from achieving complete domination, whereas nothing could be guaranteed to control men who possessed complete civil and political power. Then Question III: after establishing that equality of enjoyments depends upon equal civil rights, Thompson asks the crucial question: can equal civil rights be assured except through equal political rights?

There are those men, who, abashed at the iniquities of what is ludicrously styled the *marriage contract*, and at all the civil and moral exclusions to which women are subjected, when such matters are fairly put before them . . . still startle at the only measures which can be attended with even a chance of removing them under the present social system of individual competition for wealth. "True," they say, "the inequalities of marriage laws, the despotism of the stronger party, are nothing but the odious remains of ancient barbarism, the abuse of the superior strength of the savage. Personal protection of law, redress and punishment for offences against each other in the marriage state, as in every other, ought to be equal: women ought to have as ample means of acquiring all species of knowledge and industrious occupations as men: the disgrace ought to be abolished of sexual legislation and sexual morality awarding pernicious gratifications and impunity to men, [while awarding] to women endless privations, or destitution and death if they but touch a rose out of the heap with which man regales his bloated appetites. True, all the injustice ought to be rectified. Of two persons engaging in the same act, one ought not to be more severely punished than another. But why talk of *political* rights for women? Cannot all the barbarian laws, imposing these unequal restraints and punishments on the weaker instead of the stronger party . . . be repealed, as they were made, by *men*? If women get equal means of education, equal civil and domestic rights, equal duties and no more than equal punishments for the infraction of these duties, with men, what more would they want? Of what further use would political rights be to them, than to obtain these advantages?"

A sufficient answer to all these repentant professions would perhaps be this. "If men be sincere in the desire of affording equal enjoyments to women, in proportion to their capacity, by means of faculties equally cultivated, and other means equally ample . . . if they be sincere in the desire of yielding to women equal civil rights, as a means of procuring this equality of enjoyment—what motive could induce men so disposed still to withhold from women those political rights, which are the obvious means of procuring and preserving for them the protection of equal civil and criminal laws, the guarantee of equal chances of enjoyment? There must be some motive for this withholding, some lurking love of despotism." . . .

Again—the assumption involved in these repentant professions is not true. It is not true that all the good that can be derived to women from the possession of equal political rights with men, is the equality of civil and criminal laws between them and men. It has been shown that a second advantage, the expansion of the mind, of the intellectual powers, and of the sympathies of benevolence, depends on the exercise of these powers; and that without this comprehensiveness of mind and benevolence, some of the greatest enjoyments arising from civil equality would be lost as they would all be lessened. . . . Political rights are necessary to women as a check on the almost inveterate habits of exclusion of men. It is in vain to sanction by law a civil right, or to remove an exclusion, if the law affords no means to those whom it designs to benefit of causing the right or permission to be enforced. . . . [I]f none but men are to be jurors or judges when women complain against men of partiality and injustice, is it in human nature that a sympathy from old habit, from similarity of organization and trains of thought, from love of domination, should not have a tendency to make men swerve from the line of justice and strict impartiality, should not make them underrate the pretensions of women, and be lenient to the errors of men? When to this are joined the superior strength, the *secrecy* of domestic wrongs, and thence the means of transgression and impunity, who can doubt the necessity of an equally mixed . . . impartial, tribunal, in all cases where women are the parties as against men[?] . . . In all cases where partiality was only suspected, women would of course exercise their rights. If but few women were themselves elected as representatives, their influence would cause such men to be elected as would enact equal laws between the two great portions of the race, or would cause such men as showed an inclination to revive the old reign of brutality and injustice to be replaced by other men or by women. Now is it possible to conceive that any set of legislators, male or female, particularly men, would not be more inclined to make and preserve laws of entire reciprocity and equal justice between women and men, when they knew that their constituents were equally balanced, and that injustice on their part would necessarily enlist a few of either party amongst the injured half, and thus create a majority of the whole constituents against them? . . .

A second reason why women, in addition to equal laws and an equal system of morals, should also possess equal political rights and be eligible to all offices (if so disposed, and not by rotation or compulsion), like men, is, that exclusive legislators, particularly men as exclusive legislators for women, though ever so sincerely inclined to promote the happiness of those whom they exclude equally with their own, must be liable to errors from want of knowledge, from *false judgments*. How can exclusive legislators know the interests of those who are not their constituents, of those whom they never consult, who have no control over them? . . . What is one of the eternal excuses for iniquitous legislation, on the part of those who affect to take into consideration the influence of their measures not only on their own interests but on those also of all others liable to be affected by them? Is it not the pretence that the measures in question do really promote the interests of those whom they affect? What means so simple and effectual, what other practicable means are there, of silencing for ever this pretext, or gratifying the allegation if sincere, as affording the means of collecting by personal vote the opinions of those whose interests are at stake? Till this simple expedient is resorted to, any interests, at the will of the law-makers, may be said to be promoted by any measures. . . .

To these moral circumstances a physical circumstance is to be added, which of itself alone would demonstrate the most unqualified and indispensable necessity of political rights to women, in order to guaranty to them all the happiness which equal civil and criminal laws are calculated to afford. From the physical organization of women, as regards the bearing and rearing of children, (suppose that even the rearing terminated with weaning or at a year old,) they must, on an average, be more engaged in and more inclined to affairs of domesticity than men. Men, on an average, must, of the two, be more out of doors, more frequently mingling and associating with their fellow-creatures, more engaged in and conversant with the incidents and interests of large masses, of their country, or of society in general. Men must always have therefore superior opportunities of influence, of attaining their ends, of protecting themselves by indirect means without the protection which the direct check of political rights gives them. . . . The absolute quantity of the time of confinement during life may not, on ordinary occasions, and under improved arrangements, be much: but the *tendency* to attach too great relative importance to domestic and selfish over social and sympathetic affections, to immediate over remote objects and enjoyments, must ever (if not by wise and benevolent expedients counteracted) remain with the sex which is from physical causes the most confined. . . . The more women are isolated and stultified with their children, with their fire and food-preparing processes, the more it is necessary, though the more difficult it becomes, that they should receive illumination and comprehensiveness of mind from without, in order to counter-balance this unfavorable tendency of their situation. The sharing equally in political rights with men, and thus acquiring an interest in what concerns others more than themselves . . . is the only mode of curing the defects of character to which the organization of women renders them more prone than men, and which have a constant tendency to render them indifferent and inattentive to those remote circumstances and arrangements, those delicate agencies of laws and morals on which the possibility of acquiring happiness ultimately depends. (167–182)

Thompson is both too honest and too idealistic to end here. He must acknowledge how far women are from true political equality and must argue for a completely new form of social organization. Thompson's greatness lies in his recognition of woman's plight as one effect of a basic social ill, competition. So long as human beings battle for material gain, woman will be handicapped by her physical inferiority and man will remain brutalized by the battle. Thompson's alternative to competition is cooperation. He seeks the equal distribution of wealth in a society where all human beings contribute what they can and receive what they need. Finally, however, Thompson recognizes that so complete a reform will not occur soon. He ends his *Appeal* by urging women to take the indispensable step toward cooperation—to achieve full civil and political rights under the present system of competition.

> Still evils encompass you, inherent in the very system of labor by individual competition, even in its most free and perfect form. Men dread the competition of other men, of each other, in every line of industry. How much more will they dread your additional competition! How much will this dread of the competition of your industry and talents be aggravated by their previous contempt of your fabricated impotence! . . .
>
> An evil of no less magnitude, and immediately consequent on the preceding, opposes your happiness in the present state of social arrangements. Will man, laboring by individual competition, afford you any part of the fruits of his individual exertions as a compensation for the loss of time, pain, and expense incurred by women in bearing and rearing his and your common children? His present compensation of measured food, clothing, and idleness, with despotism over young children and inferior animals to compensate for his more lofty despotism over yourselves, coupled with personal insignificance, in what he calls his marriage contract, you know, or ought to know, how to appreciate. . . . [T]he utmost compensation you could expect from this source would never

afford you a permanent chance of happiness equal to that of men. You will always, under the system of individual competition and individual accumulations of wealth, be liable to the casualty of misery on the death of the active producer of the family, and occasional injustice from domestic abuse of superior strength and influence, against which no laws can entirely guard. Under the system of production by individual competition, it is impossible to expect that public opinion should be raised so high as to supply the defects of law, which can only repress—at the expense of the minor evils of punishment—the more flagrant and proveable acts of injustice, but can not take cognizance of those minute occurrences which so often form the groundwork of the happiness or misery of life. Superiority in the production or accumulation of individual wealth will ever be whispering into man's ear preposterous notions of his relative importance over woman, which notions must be ever prompting him to unsocial airs towards women, and particularly towards that woman who co-operates with him in the rearing of a family: for, individual wealth being under this system the one thing needful, all other qualities not tending to acquire it, though contributing ever so largely to increase the common stock of mutual happiness, are disregarded; and compensation for the exercise of such qualities or talents, for the endurance of pains and privations, would scarcely be dreamed of. . . .

Not so under the system of, Association, or of Labor by Mutual Co-operation.

This scheme of social arrangements is the only one which will complete and for ever insure the perfect equality and entire reciprocity of happiness between women and men. Those evils, which neither an equality of civil and criminal laws, nor of political laws, nor an equal system of morals upheld by an enlightened public opinion, can entirely obviate, this scheme of human exertion will remove or abundantly compensate. Even for the partial dispensations of nature it affords a remedy. Large numbers of men and women co-operating together for mutual happiness, all their possessions and means of enjoyment being the equal property of all—individual property and competition for ever excluded— women are not asked to *labor* as much in point of strength of muscle as men, but to contribute what they can, with as much cheerful benevolence, to the common happiness. All talents, all faculties, whether from nature or education, whether of mind or muscle, are here equally appreciated if they are . . . necessary to keep up the common mass of happiness. Here no dread of being deserted by a husband with a helpless and pining family, could compel a woman to submit to the barbarities of an exclusive master. . . . She is bound by no motives to submit to injustice: it would not, therefore, be practised upon her. . . . Here, the daughter of the deserted mother could not, from want or vanity, sell the use of her person. She is as fully supplied with all comforts as any other member of the community, co-operating with them in whatever way her talents may permit to the common good. The vile trade of prostitution, consigning to untimely graves the youth and beauty of every civilized land, and gloated on by men pursuing individual wealth and upholding the sexual and partial system of morals, could not here exist. Man has, here, no individual wealth more than woman, with which to buy her person for the animal use of a few years. Man, like woman, if he wish to be beloved, must learn the art of pleasing, of benevolence, of deserving love. Here, the happiness of a young woman is not blasted for life by the scorn and persecutions of unrelenting hypocrisy, for that very indiscretion which weaves the gay chaplet of exulting gallantry round the forehead of unrestrained man. Morality is, here, just and equal in her awards. Why so? Because, man having no more wealth than woman, and no more influence over the general property, and his superior strength being brought down to its just level of utility, he can procure no sexual gratification but from the voluntary affection of woman: in proscribing her indiscretions, therefore, he must proscribe his own. . . .

In the mean time, however, until the association of men and women in large numbers for mutual benefit shall supersede the present isolated mode of exertion by individual competition, assert every where your right as human beings to equal individual liberty, to equal laws, political, civil, and criminal, to equal morals, to equal education,—and, as the result of the whole, to equal chances, according to the extent and improvement of your faculties and exertions, of acquiring the means of happiness, with men. Immense would be the accession of happiness to both men and women by such a change, though it should still leave uncompensated those casualties, attended with pain and privation to you individually, but of the very highest order of utility to the whole race, to which you are exclusively subjected. . . . No wretches ever passed from a state of slavery to a state of freedom without more or less of mental excitement, without more or less of alarm to the timid amongst their masters. These are partial and necessary evils, swelling almost into blessings from the immensity of preponderant good by which they are followed. Regard them not. Truth, benevolence, the interest of the whole human race, are on your side. Persevere, and you must be free. If to your intelligence and efforts this mighty change in human affairs shall be indebted, you will lay men under an obligation of gratitude to you, in comparison with which the past use of your mere animal charms would be like the fretful dream of the morning. (197–201; 207–8)

3

Margaret Fuller and Woman in the Nineteenth Century

At the age of thirty, Margaret Fuller was "the somewhat angular Boston Sibyl";[1] at thirty-four, in New York, she was the first American newspaperwoman and a major cultural critic; at thirty-eight she was a revolutionary in Italy, with a baby and an Italian lover she may have married; at forty, returning to America with her husband and baby, she was shipwrecked within sight of shore, and drowned. At every stage of her short, brilliant career Margaret Fuller was, by choice, a public figure— a figure like that of no other nineteenth-century woman. With great energy and intellect but with no beauty or wealth, she fascinated, repelled, and ultimately perplexed her contemporaries. In 1903, Henry James portrayed her as the "Margaret-ghost" haunting his account of mid-century America.[2] And no wonder. Her life, no less than her 1845 book, *Woman in the Nineteenth Century*, claimed new identities envisioned with mythic boldness for the historical Woman. Her friends, unable to reconcile those claims with their affection for her, created a more palatable myth of a "noble," "true," and long-suffering Fuller in the widely read *Memoirs* (1852).[3] More than a century after her death in 1850, Margaret Fuller remains an uncomfortable and largely unassimilated presence in Anglo-American culture.

The discomfort she causes is, however, just what makes it difficult to omit her from any account of the Woman Question. As the author of *Woman in the Nineteenth Century* she is one of the first great voices of American feminism, if not the major Anglo-American theorist between Thompson and Mill. But her influence on Victorians is harder to assess. In nineteenth-century America her reputation as a feminist was at least as great as her reputation as a Transcendentalist and a critic. Fuller's feminism was more often mentioned with embarrassment in British periodicals, and *Woman* was not extensively reviewed or, apparently, read. The *Memoirs* version of Fuller's acts and words was far more popular. The *Memoirs* were influential in America, too, despite inconsistencies between the portrait of Fuller there and the immediate impact of Fuller and her book.[4] That impact, however, was not forgotten; it is evident even in the perplexed and tempering accounts of Emerson, Channing, and Clarke in the *Memoirs*.

Fuller did everything intensely, constantly pushing both her actions and her rhetoric to extremes. Hardly anyone could adopt her views, and no one really followed her example. But that she *was* somehow important was never in doubt. The editors of the *Memoirs* knew it; so did her detractors. Altogether too easy a target for ridicule, she provoked some of the most virulent attacks on any Victorian woman.[5] At the same time, however, that "strange, wild woman" (as Mary Russell Mitford called her)[6] stirred different feelings. Especially among women, her wildness was perceived as extraordinary bravery, and called forth unexpected and often unspecified sympathies. Elizabeth Barrett Browning tried to avoid her only to be "drawn strongly" to Fuller when they finally met. Shaken by her death, Browning could not forget the "truth and courage" of a woman whose politics and prose style she did not admire.[7] Browning's autobiographical poem *Aurora Leigh*, published six years later, is also haunted by the unnamed ghost of Margaret Fuller—Fuller lends her spirit to the heroine with whom Browning herself identified. George Eliot shunned Fuller's assertive, grandiloquent style in prose and action, but she found herself no less strongly moved to write about her when she read an account of Fuller's life.[8] Her anonymous *Leader* article of 1855, "Margaret Fuller and

Mary Wollstonecraft," is Eliot's most outspoken statement of sympathy with the ardent hopes of nineteenth-century feminism.[9] Fuller's impact on American feminists was also striking, but again half-concealed in their statements. When Elizabeth Cady Stanton and Susan B. Anthony published the first volume of their *History of Woman Suffrage*, in 1881, Fuller was only one of nineteen great precursors to whom the volume was dedicated. But though very little was said of her contributions in their text, in the tiny print of the first appendix she is "the precursor," "calling forth the opinions of her sex upon Life, Literature, Mythology, Art, Culture, and Religion. . . . She was the largest woman, and not a woman who wanted to be a man."[10]

For many who knew her, that Fuller was indeed "the largest woman" in nineteenth-century America, and said so, made sympathy with her extremely difficult. Women found her no less troubling than men, but she seems to have had upon some of them a different effect as well: the power of "calling forth . . . opinions" and sympathies which they had not before expressed. Emerson, Channing, and Clarke might portray Fuller as a noble friend, James might describe her as the Boston Sibyl, but a woman writing of her in 1884 saw her rather as "a sibyl in a straight jacket. Was it any wonder that she raved?"[11] In a sense Fuller was, as this comment implies, yet another madwoman in the attic of the Victorian imagination—yet though she was no less haunting than the hidden alter egos of women's gothic fiction, she had her existence outside the pages of Mary Shelley's or Charlotte Brontë's novels. Her sphere was history, not fiction.[12] In both her life and her book she insisted on connecting the mythic powers of women in literature with the potential powers of real women in the nineteenth century. Joining current history to old myths, the sibyl in the straitjacket became the first important voice of an apocalyptic feminism.

I

Fuller's life, even as filtered through her perplexed friends in the *Memoirs*, certainly has much to interest intellectually restless women. Like John Stuart Mill, Margaret Fuller was rigorously educated by her father. Her peers were the young men of New

England preparing for Harvard, but her formidable knowledge and abilities and her sex set her apart from them. Again like Mill, she revolted from her father's influence when she discovered Romanticism, turning to Carlyle, Goethe, and the German idealists to supplement Timothy Fuller's emphasis on history, the classics, and eighteenth-century rationalism. But Fuller's education complicated her personal development still more than Mill's. Timothy Fuller could not provide her with an intellectual community or professional tasks equal to her education, as James Mill could and did for his son. When the Fullers moved to rural Groton, Massachusetts, Margaret lost the intellectual stimulation of Cambridge; two years later, on Timothy Fuller's unexpected death, she became the *de facto* head of the family, and began teaching the next year. At thirty, Fuller looked back on her childhood as unnatural and blamed her education for her "morbid temperament" and a persistent nervousness she said would send her to a premature grave.[13] At thirty-three she was more appreciative of what her father had done for her, but still very aware of her anomalous position as an intellectual woman in America. In *Woman in the Nineteenth Century* she describes her own upbringing in that of the fictional "Miranda," to whom she turns as an example of a new breed of woman.

> I was talking . . . with Miranda, a woman, who, if any in the world could, might speak without heat and bitterness of the position of her sex. Her father was a man who cherished no sentimental reverence for Woman, but a firm belief in the equality of the sexes. She was his eldest child, and came to him at an age when he needed a companion. From the time she could speak and go alone, he addressed her not as a plaything, but as a living mind. Among the few verses he ever wrote was a copy addressed to this child, when the first locks were cut from her head; and the reverence expressed on this occasion for that cherished head, he never belied. It was to him the temple of immortal intellect. He respected his child, however, too much to be an indulgent parent. He called on her for clear judgment, for courage, for honor and fidelity; in short, for such virtues as he knew. In so far as he possessed the keys to the wonders of this universe, he allowed free use of them to her, and, by the incentive of a high expectation, he forbade, so far as possible, that she should let the privilege lie idle.
>
> Thus this child was early led to feel herself a child of the spirit. She took her place easily, not only in the world of organized being, but in the world of mind. A dignified sense of self-dependence was given as all her portion, and she found it a sure anchor. Herself

securely anchored, her relations with others were established with equal security. She was fortunate in a total absence of those charms which might have drawn to her bewildering flatteries, and in a strong electric nature, which repelled those who did not belong to her, and attracted those who did. With men and women her relations were noble,—affectionate without passion, intellectual without coldness. The world was free to her, and she lived freely in it. Outward adversity came, and inward conflict; but that faith and self-respect had early been awakened which must always lead, at last, to an outward serenity and an inward peace.

Of Miranda I had always thought as an example, that the restraints upon the sex were insuperable only to those who think them so, or who noisily strive to break them. She had taken a course of her own, and no man stood in her way. Many of her acts had been unusual, but excited no uproar. Few helped, but none checked her; and the many men who knew her mind and her life, showed to her confidence as to a brother, gentleness as to a sister. And not only refined, but very coarse men approved and aided one in whom they saw resolution and clearness of design. Her mind was often the leading one, always effective.

When I talked with her upon these matters, and had said very much what I have written, she smilingly replied: "And yet we must admit that I have been fortunate, and this should not be. My good father's early trust gave the first bias, and the rest followed, of course. It is true that I have had less outward aid, in after years, than most women; but that is of little consequence. Religion was early awakened in my soul,—a sense that what the soul is capable to ask it must attain, and that, though I might be aided and instructed by others, I must depend on myself as the only constant friend. This self-dependence, which was honored in me, is deprecated as a fault in most women. They are taught to learn their rule from without, not to unfold it from within.

"This is the fault of Man, who is still vain, and wishes to be more important to Woman than, by right, he should be."

"Men have not shown this disposition toward you," I said.

"No; because the position I early was enabled to take was one of self-reliance. And were all women as sure of their wants as I was, the result would be the same. But they are so overloaded with precepts by guardians, who think that nothing is so much to be dreaded for a woman as originality of thought or character, that their minds are impeded by doubts till they lose their chance of fair, free proportions. The difficulty is to get them to the point from which they shall naturally develop self-respect, and learn self-help.[14]

Fuller's gratitude to her father for her "self-dependence" came after four years in which she had found some measure of the identity and the community she sought. First as a school teacher in Providence and later (1839–44) as the leader of weekly "Conversations" for Boston's most highly educated women, Fuller impressed her listeners as a brilliant performer and fascinating personality, reminding them of Madame de Staël's romantic heroine, Corinne.[15] To many of her women students she was an inspiring model, an alternative to the domestic angel. To less sympathetic observers she was a formidable and slightly comic freak.[16] Fuller had also discovered a congenial intellectual community in the Transcendentalists and formed an intense and often troubled friendship with their most important member, Ralph Waldo Emerson. For two years she edited the Transcendentalist journal, *The Dial*. In July, 1843, she published there a long article which she revised and published in 1845 as *Woman in the Nineteenth Century*.

With its stress on "self-dependence" and cultivation of an inner, intellectual life, *Woman in the Nineteenth Century* reflects views which Fuller shared with the Transcendentalists. But the book also looks forward to imminent changes in Fuller's life. Travelling in the West in the summer of 1843, she noted the ambivalent attitudes of settlers toward dispossessed American Indians; in upstate New York to revise her woman article in October, 1844, she visited women prisoners at Sing-Sing and talked with the reforming warden (and later apostle of female superiority), Eliza Farnham; arriving in New York in December, 1844, she began to write reports for Horace Greeley's *New York Tribune*, not only of art and books but also of social conditions in the city. For the first time, in 1843 and 1844, she wrote with admiration of abolitionism, a subject she had once barred from her Boston "Conversations." The facts of second-class citizenship imposed by law, poverty, and prejudice increasingly absorbed her attention. Something of this new interest in social criticism is already evident in the *Dial* article, and more was included in the revised book.

The New York journalist had already begun to leave the expectations and the rhetoric of *Woman in the Nineteenth Century* behind, however. In Italy the transformation from sibyl to revolutionary was completed. When Fuller left New York in 1846 for a long-desired trip to Europe, she spent her first months surveying radical politics in Paris and urban poverty in Edinburgh, London, and Lyons (France). The apocalyptic expectations of a new era for America that echo through *Woman in the Nineteenth Century* were expanded by her growing sense of social crisis in Europe, and given a different and much more political direction by the fermentation there on the eve of the 1848 revolutions. When Fuller arrived in Italy in 1847 she was ready to commit herself to the Italian struggle for an independent republican government. Some facts of Fuller's still-obscure life in Italy are certain: she met an Italian aristocrat-turned-republican, Angelo Ossoli, had a son in September, 1848, and told friends that she had been secretly married to Ossoli; meanwhile she worked on a history of the Italian revolution, wrote articles for the *Tribune* supporting Mazzini and the Italian uprising, and during the French siege of Rome, which led to the republican defeat, managed a hospital and personally nursed the wounded. But the terms in which Fuller understood her activities are not clear. Her manuscript on the revolution was lost with her. Contemporaries viewed her actions in contradictory ways. Many New England acquaintances were shocked at her sexual behavior; others interpreted her marriage as an acceptance of the angelic ideal. Friends and enemies alike were puzzled at her choice of the gentle, unintellectual Ossoli.[17] Like Queen Victoria, Fuller seems to have found in Ossoli not just a husband-father but a full set of family relationships. Where Queen Victoria may not have been conscious of the androgynous roles she and Albert filled in their marriage, however, Fuller had written at length of an androgynous ideal in *Woman in the Nineteenth Century*. But there she had called on woman to achieve androgyny alone, putting off until the new era the mutual achievement of androgyny through marriage.

As for Fuller's political activities, the myth of the romantic heroine pursued her and suggested to some contemporaries that her revolutionary sympathies were a final romantic act, an improvised theme appropriate to an American Corinne. Elizabeth Barrett Browning, who knew her in Italy, seemed to confirm that image when she said that Fuller's writing was "just naught" —her brilliance, like Corinne's, was in conversation and personality. But Browning also said that Fuller's unfinished manuscript would be "deeply coloured by the blood colours of Socialistic views"—a radical work to be taken seriously.[18] Fuller herself hints at a political radicalism, drawn from "the cry of Communism, the systems of Fourier, etc.," which made her critical of Mazzini's romantic nationalism, and which she could not develop "in the small print of the *Tribune*."[19] Perhaps Fuller understood her marriage and motherhood not only as sexual liberation or angelic fulfillment but also as an essential part of her broader socialist convictions.[20] Restructuring the family and reorganizing society were twin goals for the Communists and Fourierists she admired. Such interpretations of Fuller's last actions can never be definitely confirmed, however. They do serve to remind us that Fuller herself may have left the views of *Woman in the Nineteenth Century* far behind. But if she did, few Victorians felt the full impact of her political and sexual radicalism. Fuller's death at forty left the meaning of her life as a woman of the nineteenth century a puzzle; the opinions she expressed in her book, however, can be more directly examined.

II

Woman in the Nineteenth Century envisions a future of almost unlimited possibilities for women. It made a great impression on those who read it in the 1840s and 1850s. Yet it was and is not an easy book to read. *Woman* combines the observations of an astute journalist with an immense and disconcertingly eclectic knowledge of Western culture and history. There is a mixture of styles as well as a proliferation of subjects—pulpit eloquence with matter-of-fact but rambling prose. What holds the book together and gives it a distinctive character is Fuller's pervasive effort to shape a positive vision. Out of the cultural traditions in which she was steeped, she constructs a different future. Shakespeare, Aeschylus, Xenophon, Judaism, Christianity, Goethe, Swedenborg, Fourier, Mme. de Roland, Mme. de Staël, Queen Elizabeth, New York State property laws, social behavior at fashionable spas, electrical theories of physiology—all provide for Fuller suggestions of undeveloped powers in women. She finds real or fictive heroines everywhere. Her heroines are all in some respect flawed or stunted. But that such women, however inadequate, have existed or been imagined indicates, for Fuller, the heroic or mythic human possibilities yet to be realized. Fuller's analyses of the constricting past and present situations of women are often acute, and her sense of injustice strong.

Claims of intellectual and spiritual equality are implicit in her vision of Woman. But the book is not an argument for legal, social, and economic equality, in the rationalist tradition of Mary Wollstonecraft, Thompson, or John Stuart Mill. Fuller's main interest is the cultivation of intellect and of psychological independence. Her suggestions range from the immediately practical to the apocalyptic. But *Woman*'s appeal is finally to the imagination. Fuller's is a vision of what the historical future might be.

For all the inward focus and the visionary hopes of *Woman*, it is also very much a document of its time. Fuller touches on most of the subjects which were or became controversies within the Woman Question. She has an alert eye for what she calls the "signs of the times," and is just as likely to incorporate cultural fashions into her vision of the future as to criticize them from her perspective as a woman. To read her in the context of the Victorian debate is to find her not only boldly imaginative but also fully embroiled in the particulars of that debate. Writing on science, for example, she uses scientistic speculations to support her view of woman's special nature:

> The electrical, the magnetic element in Woman has not been fairly brought out at any period. Everything might be expected from it; she has far more of it than Man. This is commonly expressed by saying that her intuitions are more rapid and more correct. You will often see men of high intellect absolutely stupid in regard to the atmosphere changes, the fine invisible links which connect the forms of life around them, while common women, if pure and modest, so that a vulgar self do not overshadow the mental eye, will seize and delineate these with unerring discrimination. . . . Those [women] who seem overladen with electricity frighten those [men] around them. (103, 104)

Fuller also recognizes how the physical sciences are often used against women. She attacks both the physician-psychologist and the physiologist-anthropologist.

> Among ourselves, the exhibition of such a [sexual] repugnance from a woman who had been given in marriage "by advice of friends," was treated by an eminent physician as sufficient proof of insanity. If he had said sufficient cause for it, he would have been nearer right.

History jeers at the attempts of physiologists to bind great original laws by the forms which flow from them. They make a rule; they say from observation what can and cannot be. In vain! Nature provides exceptions to every rule. She sends women to battle, and sets Hercules spinning; she enables women to bear immense burdens, cold, and frost; she enables the man, who feels maternal love, to nourish his infant like a mother. . . . Presently she will make a female Newton, and a male Syren. (152, 116)

Similarly, on the question of opening new employments to women, she can say with a fine confidence

. . . if you ask me what offices they [women] may fill, I reply—any. I do not care what case you put; let them be sea-captains, if you will. (174)

Yet she qualifies her assertion of absolute equality with an acknowledgment—like Mill's—that echoes the most conservative arguments from woman's nature:

I have no doubt, however, that a large proportion of women would give themselves to the same employments as now, because there are circumstances that must lead them. Mothers will delight to make the nest soft and warm. Nature would take care of that. (175)

Fuller appears to take sides on these and other controversial issues, but her opinions need some interpretation. She is not an activist for equal access to male institutions and opportunities—jobs, universities, the vote. But her apparent conservatism is an indication less of opposition to these reforms than of different concerns. To her predominant interest in encouraging what she calls the Minerva aspect of woman—her more "masculine" qualities—she adds an interest in exploring the Muse—those qualities like intuition traditionally regarded as the feminine virtues. It is in suggesting ways in which future women may contribute these qualities to human progress that she becomes most eloquent and most prophetic.

Throughout *Woman in the Nineteenth Century*, Fuller speaks constantly of the approach of "the new era," "the coming age," "the reign of love and peace," "an era of freedom . . . and new revelations." One source of Fuller's rhetoric is the American perfectionism of the mid-nineteenth century (augmented by Swedenborg and Fourier), and behind that, a Jeffersonian belief in America's special mission. Fuller expects the new era to begin in America. But for Fuller the new era is specifically woman's era, and her book is permeated with her vision of woman showing man the way to a fuller humanity, reforming society, and ushering in "the reign of peace and love." This vision is developed particularly in Fuller's discussions of prostitution and Christianity.

When Fuller revised her *Dial* article, she added to her main theme, the middle-class woman's need for self-dependence, a long coda on prostitution and prisoners. Her identification of woman's needs with these unwomanly women is at once a completely radical description of women's economic and sexual oppression and an appeal to one of the most sacred beliefs about woman, her moral superiority. Fuller's appeal is addressed directly to women; the call is not for self-culture this time, but for reforming action; the goal is not equality or independence, but the regeneration of a male society by women.

> I refer to the degradation of a large portion of women into the sold and polluted slaves of men, and the daring with which the legislator and man of the world lifts his head beneath the heavens, and says, "This must be; it cannot be helped; it is a necessary accompaniment of *civilization*."
>
> So speaks the *citizen*. Man born of Woman, the father of daughters, declares that he will and must buy the comforts and commercial advantages of his London, Vienna, Paris, New York, by conniving at the moral death, the damnation, so far as the action of society can insure it, of thousands of women for each splendid metropolis.
>
> O men! I speak not to you. . . . (132)
>
> But to you, women, American women, a few words may not be addressed in vain. One here and there may listen. . . . (133)
>
> A little while since I was at one of the most fashionable places of public resort. I saw there many women, dressed without regard to the season or the demands of the place, in apery, or, as it looked, in mockery, of European fashions. I saw their eyes restlessly courting attention. I saw the way in which it was paid; the style of devotion, almost an open sneer, which it pleased those ladies to receive from men whose expression marked their own low position in the moral and intellectual world. Those women went to their pillows with their heads full of folly, their hearts of jealousy, or

gratified vanity; those men, with the low opinion they already entertained of Woman confirmed. These were American *ladies*; that is, they were of that class who have wealth and leisure to make full use of the day, and confer benefits on others. They were of that class whom the possession of external advantages makes of pernicious example to many, if these advantages be misused.

Soon after, I met a circle of women, stamped by society as among the most degraded of their sex. "How," it was asked of them, "did you come here?" for by the society that I saw in the former place they were shut up in a prison. The causes were not difficult to trace: love of dress, love of flattery, love of excitement. They had not dresses like the other ladies, so they stole them; they could not pay for flattery by distinctions, and the dower of a worldly marriage, so they paid by the profanation of their persons. In excitement, more and more madly sought from day to day, they drowned the voice of conscience.

Now I ask you, my sisters, if the women at the fashionable house be not answerable for those women being in the prison? (145–46)

. . . Women are accustomed to be told by men that the reform is to come *from them.* "You," say the men, "must frown upon vice; you must decline the attentions of the corrupt; you must not submit to the will of your husband when it seems to you unworthy, but give the laws in marriage, and redeem it from its present sensual and mental pollutions."

This seems to us hard. Men have, indeed, been, for more than a hundred years, rating women for countenancing vice. But, at the same time, they have carefully hid from them its nature, so that the preference often shown by women for bad men arises rather from a confused idea that they are bold and adventurous, acquainted with regions which women are forbidden to explore, and the curiosity that ensues, than a corrupt heart in the woman. As to marriage, it has been inculcated on women, for centuries, that men have not only stronger passions than they, but of a sort that it would be shameful for them to share or even understand; that, therefore, they must "confide in their husbands," that is, submit implicitly to their will; that the least appearance of coldness or withdrawal, from whatever cause, in the wife is wicked, because liable to turn her husband's thoughts to illict indulgence; for a man is so constituted that he must indulge his passions or die!

Accordingly, a great part of women look upon men as a kind of wild beasts, but "suppose they are all alike;" the unmarried are assured by the married that, "if they knew men as they do," that is, by being married to them, "they would not expect continence or self-government from them." . . . (150–51)

On this subject, let every woman, who has once begun to think, examine herself; see whether she does not suppose virtue possible and necessary to Man, and whether she would not desire for her son a virtue which aimed at a fitness for a divine life, and involved, if not asceticism, that degree of power over the lower self, which shall "not exterminate the passions, but keep them chained at the feet of reason." The passions, like fire, are a bad master; but confine them to the hearth and the altar, and they give life to the social economy, and make each sacrifice meet for heaven.

When many women have thought upon this subject, some will be fit for the senate, and one such senate in operation would affect the morals of the civilized world.

At present I look to the young. As preparatory to the senate, I should like to see a society of novices, such as the world has never yet seen, bound by no oath, wearing no badge. In place of an oath, they should have a religious faith in the capacity of Man for virtue; instead of a badge, should wear in the heart a firm resolve not to stop short of the destiny promised him as a son of God. Their service should be action and conservatism, not of old habits, but of a better nature, enlightened by hopes that daily grow brighter.

If sin was to remain in the world, it should not be by their connivance at its stay, or one moment's concession to its claims.

They should succor the oppressed, and pay to the upright the reverence due in hero-worship by seeking to emulate them. They would not denounce the willingly bad, but they could not be with them, for the two classes could not breathe the same atmosphere.

They would heed no detention from the time-serving, the wordly and the timid.

They could love no pleasures that were not innocent and capable of good fruit. . . . (153–55)

Women of my country! . . . have you nothing to do with this? You see the men, how they are willing to sell shamelessly the happiness of countless generations of fellow-creatures, the honor of their country, and their immortal souls, for a money market and political power. Do you not feel within you that which can reprove them, which can check, which can convince them? . . . Tell them that the heart of Woman demands nobleness and honor in Man, and that, if they have not purity, have not mercy, they are no longer fathers, lovers, husbands, sons of yours. . . . This cause is your own. (166–67)

Fuller's choice of prostitution as the issue on which to arouse women to social action was prophetic and influential. The same attitude toward men, prostitutes, and their middle-class sisters is expressed by Fuller's former pupil, Caroline Dall, in the late 1850s, fuels Josephine Butler's English crusade in the 1870s, and gives the first impetus to the Purity Reform Movement that sweeps America in the last three decades of the century (see Volume II, Chapter 3). For Fuller as for later Victorians, social criticism of prostitution was one route to apocalyptic feminism.

The other route was a reexamination of woman's role as defined by religion, and here too *Woman in the Nineteenth Century* is representative and influential. Fuller addresses three of the most important issues of this aspect of the Woman Question: Genesis, woman's relation to Christianity, and female ministry (see Volume II, Chapter 4). She attacks the Adam of Genesis as severely as most feminists did, but she also sees the other side.

> The rude man, just disengaged from the sod, the Adam, accuses Woman to his God, and records her disgrace to their posterity. He is not ashamed to write that he could be drawn from heaven by one beneath him,—one made, he says, from but a small part of himself. But in the same nation, educated by time, instructed by a succession of prophets, we find Woman in as high a position as she has ever occupied. (55–56)

Fuller is equally complex about the New Testament. She attacks one of Christianity's most hallowed assumptions—that it, more than any other force in history, has elevated woman. "The Man most habitually narrow towards Woman will be flushed, as by the worst assault on Christianity, if you say it has made no improvement in her condition. Indeed, those most opposed to new acts in her favor, are jealous of the reputation of those [acts] which have been done" (48). Fuller will not, on the other hand, minimize woman's debt to Christianity. "No figure that has ever arisen to greet our eyes has been received with more fervent reverence than that of the Madonna. . . . this holy and significant image . . . exercised an immediate influence on the destiny of the sex" (56). Like many Victorians, Fuller recognizes that "Women are, indeed, the easy victims both of priestcraft and self-delusion" and that they can be rescued only "if the intellect . . . [is] developed in proportion of the other powers" (105). But, once this is done, Fuller, like the most forward-looking Christians, sees an exalted role for woman in the new church. "Man and Woman share an angelic ministry" (123). As a proponent of female ministry, Fuller does more than defend such contemporary Protestant preachers as Angelina Grimké, Abby Kelly, and Mother Anne Lee. She, like Newman, Conway, Henry Adams, Catherine Booth, and many other Victorian Christians, comes surprisingly close to Catholicism in her vision of the ministering woman as intercessor. "He [the Italian poet] did not look upon her [woman] as between him and earth, to serve his temporal needs, but, rather, betwixt him and heaven, to purify his affections and lead him to wisdom through love. He sought, in her, not so much the Eve as the Madonna" (69). Woman as Madonna is indeed the salvation of the race.

> Mysticism, which may be defined as the brooding soul of the world, cannot fail of its oracular promise as to Woman. "The mothers," "The mother of all things," are expressions of thought which lead the mind towards this side of universal growth. Whenever a mystical whisper was heard, from Behmen down to St. Simon, sprang up the thought, that, if it be true, as the legend says, that Humanity withers through a fault committed by and a curse laid upon Woman, through her pure child, or influence, shall the new Adam, the redemption, arise. Innocence is to be replaced by virtue, dependence by a willing submission, in the heart of the Virgin-Mother of the new race. (102)

In Fuller's vision of woman, the wife and mother as an angel in the house is transformed into a Virgin Mother, a pure, independent woman whose maternal love and spiritual gifts, joined to a developed intellect, make her not only the perfected Woman, but model and instrument of a perfected humanity. This vision stirred women in the coming decades fully as much as did the egalitarian ideal. From Caroline Dall to Eliza Farnham (whose *Woman and Her Era* was published in 1864), from Barbara Bodichon to Josephine Butler, Frances Willard, and Elizabeth Cady Stanton, Fuller's apocalyptic feminism is a central theme for women activists who contribute to the Woman Question.

III

Woman in the Nineteenth Century

. . . a new manifestation is at hand, a new hour in the day of Man. We cannot expect to see any one sample of completed being, when the mass of men still lie engaged in the sod, or use the freedom of their limbs only with wolfish energy. The tree cannot come to flower till its root be free from the cankering worm, and its whole growth open to air and light. While any one is base, none can be entirely free and noble. Yet something new shall presently be shown of the life of man, for hearts crave, if minds do not know how to ask it. . . . (20-21)

Meanwhile, not a few believe, and men themselves have expressed the opinion, that the time is come when Eurydice is to call for an Orpheus, rather than Orpheus for Eurydice; that the idea of Man, however imperfectly brought out, has been far more so than that of Woman; that she, the other half of the same thought, the other chamber of the heart of life, needs now take her turn in the full pulsation, and that improvement in the daughters will best aid in the reformation of the sons of this age.

It should be remarked that, as the principle of liberty is better understood, and more nobly interpreted, a broader protest is made in behalf of Woman. As men become aware that few men have had a fair chance, they are inclined to say that no women have had a fair chance. . . . The French revolution, that strangely disguised angel, bore witness in favor of woman, but interpreted her claims no less ignorantly than those of man. . . . The same tendencies, further unfolded, will bear good fruit in this country. (23-25)

. . . Of all its banners, none has been more steadily upheld, and under none have more valor and willingness for real sacrifices been shown, than that of the champions of the enslaved African. And this band it is, which, partly from a natural following out of principles, partly because many women have been prominent in that cause, makes, just now, the warmest appeal in behalf of Woman.

"Is it not enough," cries the irritated trader, "that you have done all you could to break up the national union, and thus destroy the prosperity of our country, but now you must be trying to break up family union, to take my wife away from the cradle and the kitchen-hearth to vote at polls, and preach from a pulpit? Of course, if she does such things, she cannot attend to those of her own sphere. She is happy enough as she is. She has more leisure than I have,—every means of improvement, every indulgence."

"Have you asked her whether she was satisfied with these *indulgences?*"

"No, but I know she is. She is too amiable to desire what would make me unhappy, and too judicious to wish to step beyond the sphere of her sex. I will never consent to have our peace disturbed by any such discussions."

"'Consent—you?' it is not consent from you that is in question —it is assent from your wife."

"Am not I the head of my house?"

"You are not the head of your wife. God has given her a mind of her own."

"I am the head, and she the heart."

"God grant you play true to one another, then! I suppose I am to be grateful that you did not say she was only the hand. If the head represses no natural pulse of the heart, there can be no question as to your giving your consent. Both will be of one accord, and there needs but to present any question to get a full and true answer. There is no need of precaution, of indulgence, nor consent. But our doubt is whether the heart *does* consent with the head, or only obeys its decrees with a passiveness that precludes the exercise of its natural powers, or a repugnance that turns sweet qualities to bitter, or a doubt that lays waste the fair occasions of life. It is to ascertain the truth that we propose some liberating measures."

Thus vaguely are these questions proposed and discussed at present. But their being proposed at all implies much thought, and suggests more. Many women are considering within themselves what they need that they have not, and what they can have if they find they need it. Many men are considering whether women are capable of being and having more than they are and have, *and* whether, if so, it will be best to consent to improvement in their condition. . . . (28–30)

Knowing that there exists in the minds of men a tone of feeling toward women as toward slaves, such as is expressed in the common phrase, "Tell that to women and children" . . . can we wonder that many reformers think that measures are not likely to be taken in behalf of women, unless their wishes could be publicly represented by women?

"That can never be necessary," cry the other side. "All men are privately influenced by women; each has his wife, sister, or female friends, and is too much biased by these relations to fail of representing their interests; and, if this is not enough, let them propose and enforce their wishes with the pen. The beauty of home would be destroyed, the delicacy of the sex be violated, the dignity of halls of legislation degraded, by an attempt to introduce them there. Such duties are inconsistent with those of a mother;" and then we have ludicrous pictures of ladies in hysterics at the polls, and senate-chambers filled with cradles.

But if, in reply, we admit as truth that Woman seems destined by nature rather for the inner circle, we must add that the arrangements of civilized life have not been, as yet, such as to secure it to her. Her circle, if the duller, is not the quieter. If kept from "excitement," she is not from drudgery. Not only the Indian squaw carries the burdens of the camp, but the favorites of Louis XIV accompany him in his journeys, and the washerwoman stands at her tub, and carries home her work at all seasons, and in all states of health. Those who think the physical circumstances of Woman would make a part in the affairs of national government unsuitable, are by no means those who think it impossible for negresses to endure field-work, even during pregnancy, or for sempstresses to go through their killing labors.

As to the use of the pen, there was quite as much opposition to Woman's possessing herself of that help to free agency as there is now to her seizing on the rostrum or the desk; and she is likely to draw, from a permission to plead her cause that way, opposite inferences to what might be wished by those who now grant it.

As to the possibility of her filling with grace and dignity any such position, we should think those who had seen the great actresses, and heard the Quaker preachers of modern times, would not doubt that Woman can express publicly the fulness of thought and creation, without losing any of the peculiar beauty of her sex. What can pollute and tarnish is to act thus from any motive except that something needs to be said or done. Woman could take part in the processions, the songs, the dances of old religion; no one fancied her delicacy was impaired by appearing in public for such a cause.

As to her home, she is not likely to leave it more than she now does for balls, theatres, meetings for promoting missions, revival meetings, and others to which she flies, in hope of an animation for her existence commensurate with what she sees enjoyed by men. Governors of ladies'-fairs are no less engrossed by such a charge, than the governor of a state by his; presidents of Washingtonian societies no less away from home than presidents of conventions. If men look straitly to it, they will find that, unless their lives are domestic, those of the women will not be. A house is no home unless it contain food and fire for the mind as well as for the body. . . .

As to men's representing women fairly at present, . . . when not one man, in the million, shall I say? no, not in the hundred million, can rise above the belief that Woman was made *for Man*,— when such traits as these are daily forced upon the attention, can we feel that Man will always do justice to the interests of Woman? Can we think that he takes a sufficiently discerning and religious view of her office and destiny *ever* to do her justice, except when prompted by sentiment,—accidentally or transiently, that is, for the sentiment will vary according to the relations in which he is placed? The lover, the poet, the artist, are likely to view her nobly. The father and the philosopher have some chance of liberality; the man of the world, the legislator for expediency, none.

Under these circumstances, without attaching importance, in

themselves, to the changes demanded by the champions of Woman, we hail them as signs of the times. We would have every arbitrary barrier thrown down. We would have every path laid open to Woman as freely as to Man. Were this done, and a slight temporary fermentation allowed to subside, we should see crystallizations more pure and of more various beauty. We believe the divine energy would pervade nature to a degree unknown in the history of former ages, and that no discordant collision, but a ravishing harmony of the spheres, would ensue.

Yet, then and only then will mankind be ripe for this, when inward and outward freedom for Woman as much as for Man shall be acknowledged as a *right*, not yielded as a concession. As the friend of the negro assumes that one man cannot by right hold another in bondage, so should the friend of Woman assume that Man cannot by right lay even well-meant restrictions on Woman. If the negro be a soul, if the woman be a soul, apparelled in flesh, to one Master only are they accountable. There is but one law for souls, and, if there is to be an interpreter of it, he must come not as man, or son of man, but as son of God.

Were thought and feeling once so far elevated that Man should esteem himself the brother and friend, but nowise the lord and tutor, of Woman,—were he really bound with her in equal worship,—arrangements as to function and employment would be of no consequence. What Woman needs is not as a woman to act or rule, but as a nature to grow, as an intellect to discern, as a soul to live freely and unimpeded, to unfold such powers as were given her when we left our common home. If fewer talents were given her, yet if allowed the free and full employment of these, so that she may render back to the giver his own with usury, she will not complain; nay, I dare to say she will bless and rejoice in her earthly birth-place, her earthly lot. . . . (33–38)

It is not the transient breath of poetic incense that women want; each can receive that from a lover. It is not life-long sway; it needs but to become a coquette, a shrew, or a good cook, to be sure of that. It is not money, nor notoriety, nor the badges of authority which men have appropriated to themselves. If demands, made in their behalf, lay stress on any of these particulars, those who make them have not searched deeply into the need. The want is for that which at once includes these and precludes them; which would not be forbidden power, lest there be temptation to steal and misuse it; which would not have the mind perverted by flattery from a worthiness of esteem; it is for that which is the birthright of every being capable of receiving it,—the freedom, the religious, the intelligent freedom of the universe to use its means, to learn its secret, as far as Nature has enabled them, with God alone for their guide and their judge.

Ye cannot believe it, men; but the only reason why women ever assume what is more appropriate to you, is because you prevent them from finding out what is fit for themselves. Were they free, were they wise fully to develop the strength and beauty of Woman; they would never wish to be men, or man-like. The well-instructed moon flies not from her orbit to seize on the glories of her partner. No; for she knows that one law rules, one heaven contains, one universe replies to them alike. It is with women as with the slave.

"Tremble not before the free man, but before the slave who has chains to break." (62-63)

. . . civilized Europe is still in a transition state about marriage; not only in practice but in thought. It is idle to speak with contempt of the nations where polygamy is an institution, or seraglios a custom, while practices far more debasing haunt, well-nigh fill, every city and every town, and so far as union of one with one is believed to be the only pure form of marriage, a great majority of societies and individuals are still doubtful whether the earthly bond must be a meeting of souls, or only supposes a contract of convenience and utility. Were Woman established in the rights of an immortal being, this could not be. . . .

What deep communion, what real intercourse is implied in sharing the joys and cares of parentage, when any degree of equality is admitted between the parties! It is true that, in a majority of instances, the man looks upon his wife as an adopted child, and places her to the other children in the relation of nurse or governess, rather than that of parent. Her influence with them is sure; but she misses the education which should enlighten that influence, by being thus treated. It is the order of nature that children should complete the education, moral and mental, of parents, by making them think what is needed for the best culture of human beings, and conquer all faults and impulses that interfere with their giving this to these dear objects, who represent the world to them. Father and mother should assist one another to learn what is required for this sublime priesthood of Nature. But, for this, a religious recognition of equality is required. . . . (70-72)

Too much is said of women being better educated, that they may become better companions and mothers *for men*. They should be fit for such companionship, and we have mentioned, with satisfaction, instances where it has been established. Earth knows no fairer, holier relation than that of a mother. It is one which, rightly understood, must both promote and require the highest attainments. But a being of infinite scope must not be treated with an exclusive view to any one relation. Give the soul free course, let the organization, both of body and mind, be freely developed, and the being will be fit for any and every relation to which it may be called. The intellect, no more than the sense of hearing, is to be cultivated merely that Woman may be a more valuable companion to Man, but because the Power who gave a power, by its mere existence signifies that it must be brought out toward perfection.

In this regard of self-dependence, and a greater simplicity and fulness of being, we must hail as a preliminary the increase of the class contemptuously designated as "old maids." . . . Not "needing to care that she [the old maid] may please a husband," a frail and limited being, her thoughts may turn to the centre, and she may, by steadfast contemplation entering into the secret of truth and love, use it for the good of all men, instead of a chosen few, and interpret through it all the forms of life. . . . (95-98)

Even among the North American Indians, a race of men as completely engaged in mere instinctive life as almost any in the world, and where each chief, keeping many wives as useful servants, of course looks with no kind eye on celibacy in Woman, it was excused in the following instance mentioned by Mrs. Jameson. A woman dreamt in youth that she was betrothed to the Sun. She built her a wigwam apart, filled it with emblems of her alliance, and means of an independent life. There she passed her days, sustained by her own exertions, and true to her supposed engagement.

In any tribe, we believe, a woman, who lived as if she was betrothed to the Sun, would be tolerated, and the rays which made her youth blossom sweetly, would crown her with a halo in age.

There is, on this subject, a nobler view than heretofore, if not the noblest, and improvement here must coincide with that in the view taken of marriage. "We must have units before we can have union," says one of the ripe thinkers of the times. . . . (101)

All these motions of the time, tides that betoken a waxing moon, overflow upon our land. The world at large is readier to let Woman learn and manifest the capacities of her nature than it ever was before, and here is a less encumbered field and freer air than anywhere else. And it ought to be so; we ought to pay for Isabella's jewels.

The names of nations are feminine—Religion, Virtue and Victory are feminine. To those who have a superstition, as to outward reigns, it is not without significance that the name of the queen of our mother-land should at this crisis be Victoria,—

Victoria the First. Perhaps to us it may be given to disclose the era thus outwardly presaged. . . .

In our own country, women are, in many respects, better situated than men. Good books are allowed, with more time to read them. They are not so early forced into the bustle of life, nor so weighed down by demands for outward success. The perpetual changes, incident to our society, make the blood circulate freely through the body politic, and, if not favorable at present to the grace and bloom of life, they are so to activity, resource, and would be to reflection, but for a low materialist tendency, from which the women are generally exempt in themselves, though its existence, among the men, has a tendency to repress their impulses and make them doubt their instincts, thus often paralyzing their action during the best years.

But they have time to think, and no traditions chain them, and few conventionalities, compared with what must be met in other nations. There is no reason why they should not discover that the secrets of nature are open, the revelations of the spirit waiting, for whoever will seek them. When the mind is once awakened to this consciousness, it will not be restrained by the habits of the past, but fly to seek the seeds of a heavenly future. (107–9)

There are two aspects of Woman's nature, represented by the ancients as Muse and Minerva. . . .

The especial genius of Woman I believe to be electrical in movement, intuitive in function, spiritual in tendency. She excels not so easily in classification, or recreation, as in an instinctive seizure of causes, and a simple breathing out of what she receives, that has the singleness of life, rather than the selecting and energizing of art.

More native is it to her to be the living model of the artist than to set apart from herself any one form in objective reality; more native to inspire and receive the poem, than to create it. In so far as soul is in her completely developed, all soul is the same; but in so far as it is modified in her as Woman, it flows, it breathes, it sings, rather than deposits soil, or finishes work; and that which is especially feminine flushes, in blossom, the face of earth, and pervades, like air and water, all this seeming solid globe, daily renewing and purifying its life. Such may be the especially feminine element spoken of as Femality. But it is no more the order of nature that it should be incarnated pure in any form, than that the masculine energy should exist unmingled with it in any form.

Male and female represent the two sides of the great radical dualism. But, in fact, they are perpetually passing into one another. Fluid hardens to solid, solid rushes to fluid. There is no wholly masculine man, no purely feminine woman. . . .

CAMROSE LUTHERAN COLLEGE
LIBRARY

Men partake of the feminine in the Apollo; women of the masculine as Minerva.

What I mean by the Muse is that unimpeded clearness of the intuitive powers, which a perfectly truthful adherence to every admonition of the higher instincts would bring to a finely organized human being. It may appear as prophecy or as poesy. It enabled Cassandra to foresee the results of actions passing round her; the Seeress to behold the true character of the person through the mask of his customary life. (Sometimes she saw a feminine form behind the man, sometimes the reverse.) . . . It gave a man, but a poet-man, the power of which he thus speaks: "Often in my contemplation of nature, radiant intimations, and as it were sheaves of light, appear before me as to the facts of cosmogony, in which my mind has, perhaps, taken especial part." He wisely adds, "but it is necessary with earnestness to verify the knowledge we gain by these flashes of light." And none should forget this. Sight must be verified by light before it can deserve the honors of piety and genius. Yet sight comes first, and of this sight of the world of causes, this approximation to the region of primitive motions, women I hold to be especially capable. Even without equal freedom with the other sex, they have already shown themselves so; and should these faculties have free play, I believe they will open new, deeper and purer sources of joyous inspiration than have as yet refreshed the earth.

Let us be wise, and not impede the soul. Let her work as she will. Let us have one creative energy, one incessant revelation. Let it take what form it will, and let us not bind it by the past to man or woman, black or white. Jove sprang from Rhea, Pallas from Jove. So let it be.

If it has been the tendency of these remarks to call Woman rather to the Minerva side,—if I, unlike the more generous writer, have spoken from society no less than the soul,—let it be pardoned! It is love that has caused this,—love for many incarcerated souls, that might be freed, could the idea of religious self-dependence be established in them, could the weakening habit of dependence on others be broken up. . . .

It is, therefore, only in the present crisis that the preference is given to Minerva. The power of continence must establish the legitimacy of freedom, the power of self-poise the perfection of motion.

Every relation, every gradation of nature is incalculably precious, but only to the soul which is poised upon itself, and to whom no loss, no change, can bring dull discord, for it is in harmony with the central soul.

If any individual live too much in relations, so that he becomes a stranger to the resources of his own nature, he falls, after a while, into a distraction, or imbecility, from which he can only be cured by a time of isolation, which gives the renovating fountains time to rise up. With a society it is the same. Many minds, deprived of the traditionary or instinctive means of passing a cheerful existence, must find help in self-impulse, or perish. It is therefore that, while any elevation, in the view of union, is to be hailed with joy, we shall not decline celibacy as the great fact of the time. It is one from which no vow, no arrangement, can at present save a thinking mind. For now the rowers are pausing on their oars; they wait a change before they can pull together. All tends to illustrate the thought of a wise cotemporary. Union is only possible to those who are units. To be fit for relations in time, souls, whether of Man or Woman, must be able to do without them in the spirit.

It is therefore that I would have Woman lay aside all thought, such as she habitually cherishes, of being taught and led by men. I would have her, like the Indian girl, dedicate herself to the Sun, the Sun of Truth, and go nowhere if his beams did not make clear the path. I would have her free from compromise, from complaisance, from helplessness, because I would have her good enough and strong enough to love one and all beings, from the fulness, not the poverty of being.

Men, as at present instructed, will not help this work, because they also are under the slavery of habit. . . .

Men do *not* look at both sides, and women must leave off asking them and being influenced by them, but retire within themselves, and explore the ground-work of life till they find their peculiar secret. Then, when they come forth again, renovated and baptized, they will know how to turn all dross to gold, and will be rich and free though they live in a hut, tranquil if in a crowd. Then their sweet singing shall not be from passionate impulse, but the lyrical overflow of a divine rapture, and a new music shall be evolved from this many-chorded world.

Grant her, then, for a while, the armor and the javelin. Let her put from her the press of other minds, and meditate in virgin loneliness. The same idea shall reappear in due time as Muse, or Ceres, the all-kindly, patient Earth-Spirit. . . . (115–21)

I have urged on Women independence of Man, not that I do not think the sexes mutually needed by one another, but because in Woman this fact has led to an excessive devotion, which has cooled love, degraded marriage, and prevented either sex from being what it should be to itself or the other.

I wish Woman to live, *first* for God's sake. Then she will not make an imperfect man her god, and thus sink to idolatry. Then she will not take what is not fit for her from a sense of weakness and poverty. Then, if she finds what she needs in Man embodied, she will know how to love, and be worthy of being loved.

By being more a soul, she will not be less Woman, for nature is perfected through spirit.

Now there is no woman, only an overgrown child.

That her hand may be given with dignity, she must be able to stand alone. . . .

A profound thinker has said, "No married woman can represent the female world, for she belongs to her husband. The idea of Woman must be represented by a virgin."

But that is the very fault of marriage, and of the present relation between the sexes, that the woman *does* belong to the man, instead of forming a whole with him. Were it otherwise, there would be no such limitation to the thought.

Woman, self-centered, would never be absorbed by any relation; it would be only an experience to her as to man. It is a vulgar error that love, *a* love, to Woman is her whole existence; she also is born for Truth and Love in their universal energy. Would she but assume her inheritance, Mary would not be the only virgin mother. Not Manzoni alone would celebrate in his wife the virgin mind with the maternal wisdom and conjugal affections. The soul is ever young, ever virgin.

And will not she soon appear?—the woman who shall vindicate their birthright for all women; who shall teach them what to claim, and how to use what they obtain? Shall not her name be for her era Victoria, for her country and life Virginia? Yet predictions are rash; she herself must teach us to give her the fitting name. (175–77)

4

Queen Victoria and "The Shadow Side"

One way to correct modern notions of what "Victorian" means is to correct our notion of who Victoria was. Recent biographies of the Queen have not altered her popular image as archetypic Wife-Mother, the heavy angel of the house.[1] In correcting this image we must not destroy it entirely. Only by resisting the temptation to replace one inadequate extreme with another can we understand why Victoria, for all her simplicities, is representative of the conflictive era named after her.

Most conflicting elements of the era and the Queen pervade her youth. Inheriting the passionate (not to say licentious) blood of the Hanoverians, Victoria also imbibes from her milieu that penchant for prudery which is called "Victorian" and was in fact pervasive decades before 1837. Victoria's early years affect profoundly her later relationship with Albert—and with herself as a woman. Her father, the Duke of Kent, dies when Victoria is three. She subsequently seeks father-figures with an intensity which can only be called passionate: first, her uncle Leopold; then Melbourne. When King William IV dies in 1837, the succession passes to a shy young woman who feels socially and intellectually inadequate. Queen Victoria writes years later to her daughter, Vicky, that

I had no scope for my very violent feelings of affection—had no brothers and sisters to live with—never had had a father—from my unfortunate circumstances was not on a comfortable or at all intimate or confidential footing with my mother (so different from you to me)—much as I love her now—and did not know what a happy domestic life was! All this is the complete contrast to your happy childhood and home. Consequently I owe everything to dearest Papa [Albert]. He was my father, my protector, my guide and adviser in all and everything, my mother (I might almost say)as well as my husband. I suppose no-one ever was so completely altered and changed in every way as I was by dearest Papa's blessed influence.[2]

The intensity of this marriage and its ambivalences ("mother" Albert will be discussed later) indicate why the popular image of the Queen must be modified but not destroyed. She represents her era so adequately because the conflicting elements of her personality characterize the age itself. Victoria sustains both traditional reverence for the Wife-Mother and unconventional reservations about that ideal.

First, Victorian orthodoxy.

I

When Albert accepts her proposal of marriage in 1839, Victoria expresses her joy in most conventional terms.

Oh! to *feel* I was, and am, loved by *such* an Angel as Albert was *too great delight to describe*! he is *perfection*; perfection in every way—in beauty—in everything! I told him I was quite unworthy of him and kissed his dear hand—he said he would be very happy "das Leben mit dir zu zubringen" [to share life with you] and was so kind and seemed so happy, that I really felt it was the happiest brightest moment in my life, which made up for all I had suffered and endured. Oh! *how* I adore and love him, I cannot say!! *how* I will strive to make him feel as little as possible the great sacrifice he has made; I told him it was a great sacrifice,—which he wouldn't allow. . . . I feel the happiest of human beings.[3]

Victoria delights in calling Albert her lord and master; she is the one who insists upon retaining the word "obey" in the marriage service. After the ceremony Victoria continues to react most conventionally. Like the heroine of a melodrama,

I had such a sick headache that I could eat nothing, and was obliged to lie down . . . for the remainder of the evening on the sofa; but ill or not, I _never, never_ spent such an evening!! My _dearest dearest dear_ Albert sat on a footstool by my side, and his excessive love and affection gave me feelings of heavenly love and happiness I never could have _hoped_ to have felt before! He clasped me in his arms, and we kissed each other again and again! His beauty, his sweetness and gentleness—really how can I ever be thankful enough to have such a _Husband_! . . . to be called by names of tenderness, I have never yet heard used to me before—was bliss beyond belief! Oh! this was the happiest day of my life!—May God help me to do my duty as I ought and be worthy of such blessings![4]

Two weeks later her desires remain eminently proper. "God knows how great my wish is to make this beloved being happy and contented."[5] After four years and four children, Victoria portrays her bliss in a tableau which had occurred and would recur obsessively in the literature and art of the age.

The children again with us, & such a pleasure & interest! Bertie & Alice are the greatest friends & always playing together.—Later we both read to each other. When I read, I sit on a sofa, in the middle of the room, with a small table before it, on which stand a lamp & candlestick, Albert sitting in a low armchair, on the opposite side of the table with another small table in front of him on which he usually stands his book. Oh! if I could only exactly describe our dear happy life together![6]

In 1849 the intensity and conventionality of her bliss continue. "How happy we are here! And never do I enjoy myself more, or more peacefully than when I can be so much with my beloved Albert & follow him everywhere!"[7] When she later acknowledges to Vicky that Albert "completely altered and changed [me] in every way," Victoria is in fact attesting to the propriety of her marriage. To make the beloved into a "perfect lady" is a basic dream and drive of the Victorian male. Firmly if carefully, Albert reeducates Victoria in household management, in art appreciation, in handling the artisan class. He also contributes incalculably to the one aspect of her life which distinguishes Victoria from every other woman in England—her role as monarch of Europe's vastest empire. Victoria's conventional belief that "we women are not made for governing" is supported by Melbourne, who applauds her engagement: "You'll be much more comfortable, for a woman cannot stand alone for long, in whatever situation she is."[8] Victoria was indeed fortunate in her spouse. Though not without some evident reservation, she could say by 1852:

> Albert grows daily fonder and fonder of politics and business, and is so wonderfully *fit* for both—such perspicacity and such *courage*—and I grow daily to dislike them both more and more. . . .
> . . . Albert becomes really a *terrible* man of business; I think it takes a little off from the gentleness of his character, and makes him so preoccupied. I grieve over all this, as I *cannot* enjoy these things, *much* as I interest myself in *general* European politics; but I am every day more convinced that *we women, if we are* to be *good* women, *feminine* and *amiable* and *domestic*, are *not fitted to reign;* at least it is *contre gré* that they drive themselves to the *work* which it entails.
> However, this cannot now be helped, and it is the duty of every one to fulfil all that they are called upon to do, in whatever situation they may be![9]

With Albert assisting her as monarch and wife-mother, Victoria achieves a domestic situation which she consciously opposes to the licentiousness of the court and which her era and our own have considered the ideal of mid-century domesticity. (Not only did Mrs. Ellis dedicate to Queen Victoria the enormously popular *The Wives of England*, but a British matron supposedly exclaimed after seeing Sarah Bernhardt's Cleopatra, "How unlike, how very unlike, the home life of our own dear Queen."[10]) In 1860 Victoria can say of her twenty wedded years:

> Where could I point to another woman who after 20 years of such marital felicity still possesses it? My dearly beloved Albert shows me not only as much affection and kindness as ever, but as much love and tenderness as on the first day of our marriage. How can I ever repay him for it? How be sufficiently thankful to God for His goodness? And I must also count as a blessing the love of our many good children! For this truly rejoices the hearts of parents who only desire their children's welfare.[11]

These are portentous words, both because of Victoria's estimate of marriage generally and because of Albert's death six months later. Although Victoria's mourning is protracted enough to warrant the contemporary and modern charges of self-

THE WOMAN QUESTION—DEFINING VOICES

3. Victoria and Albert
Roger Fenton, 1854

indulgence, she is less idiosyncratic, more representative and conventional, than people today recognize. The Queen is very Victorian in her feeling that a wife belongs so completely to her husband that her life ends in some sense with his. Moreover, Victoria's was an era which countenanced and indeed revelled in spectacular grief—as the protracted deathbed scenes of literature and the ubiquitous ads for funeral attire attest. In the profuseness of her emotions and in the conventional expression of them, Victoria is responding as a good widow should.

> I do not even know if it is one day or seven weeks since I lost him, my hero, my glorious and exceptionally great husband, at the peak of his power and vigour, in the very prime of life! My life and thoughts depended entirely on him; my own ambition was to please him, to be worthy of him! The burdens, worries and difficulties of my position, which never had an attraction for me, were made bearable through his goodness, his wisdom and his guidance. . . .
> . . . My only comfort is the hope that I may soon be able to follow him and then be united with him for ever! . . .
> . . . I still listen in the hope that he may yet come in, his door may open and his angelic form will and must return, as so often before, from his shooting. I could go mad from the desire and longing! . . . My only desire is to continue as He, my beloved Angel, would have wished—and yet . . . I would almost rather sit and weep and live only with Him in spirit and take no interest in the things of this earth, for I believe that I am going further away from him and do not always see things so clearly as I used to! But I suppose that is God's will and one must acquiesce in that also. . . .
> My political and queenly tasks are the hardest for me.
> . . . More than ever do I long to lead a private life tending the poor and sick: I only do wearisome things with the thought that it is good in his eyes, and when I know and feel that I can promote good, maintain order, prevent evil and advance the general welfare; then I am prepared to continue so long as my weak and shattered nerves endure. . . .[12]

With so orthodox an attitude toward woman's duties, Victoria inevitably opposes Woman's Rights. She writes in 1870 to Sir Theodore Martin whom she had chosen as Albert's biographer:

> The Queen is most anxious to enlist every one who can speak or write to join in checking this mad, wicked folly of "Woman's

Rights", with all its attendant horrors, on which her poor feeble sex is bent, forgetting every sense of womanly feeling and propriety. Lady —— ought to get a *good whipping*.

It is a subject which makes the Queen so furious that she cannot contain herself. God created men and women different—then let them remain each in their own position. Tennyson has some beautiful lines on the difference of men and women in *The Princess* [III,3]. Woman would become the most hateful, heathen, and disgusting of human beings were she allowed to unsex herself; and where would be the protection which man was intended to give the weaker sex? The Queen is sure that Mrs. Martin agrees with her.[13]

Earlier the same year, Prime Minister Gladstone receives a terser but no less definite letter when he sends the Queen a pamphlet "in resolute defense of the old social ideas of Christendom on that great [woman's rights] subject." "The Queen thanks Mr. Gladstone for his 2 letters & for the pamphlet w^h is *sure* to meet with her *sympathy* as *she has* the strongest aversion for the *socalled & most erroneous 'Rights of Woman.'*"[14] Victoria is particularly adamant against women entering the medical profession, as she indicates to Gladstone in May of 1870:

> . . . The circumstances respecting the Bill to give women the same position as men with respect to Parliamentary franchise gives her an opportunity to observe that she had for some time past wished to call Mr. Gladstone's attention to the mad & utterly demoralizing movement of the present day to place women in the same position as to professions—as *men;*—& amongst others, in the *Medical Line* . . . she is *most* anxious that it sh^{ld} be known how she not only disapproves but *abhors* the attempts to destroy all propriety & womanly feeling w^h will inevitably be the result of what has been proposed. The Queen is a woman herself—& knows what an anomaly her *own* position is:—but that can be reconciled with reason & propriety tho' it is a terribly difficult & trying one. But to tear away all the barriers w^h surround a woman, & to propose that they sh^{ld} study with *men*—things w^h c^{ld} not be named before them—certainly not *in a mixed* audience—w^{ld} be to introduce a total disregard of what must be considered as belonging to the rules & principles of morality.
>
> The Queen feels so strongly upon this dangerous & unchristian & unnatural *cry* & movement of "woman's rights,"—in w^h she knows Mr. Gladstone *agrees*, (as he sent her that excellent Pamphlet by a Lady) that she is most anxious that Mr. Gladstone

& others sh^{ld} take some steps to check this alarming danger & to make whatever use they can of her name. . . .

Let woman be what God intended; a helpmate for a man—but with totally different duties & vocations.

The Queen is glad that the Govt will support Mr. Bouverie's motion—but she *feels* the danger as regards the subject she attended to to be so *vy serious* that she is determined for the *salvation* of the *young women* of this country—& their *rescue* from *immorality* to do *every* thing she *can* to put a check to it.—She wishes Mr. Gladstone w^{ld} send for & see Sir Wm Jenner who can tell him what an *awful* idea this is—of allowing *young girls* & young men to *enter* the dissecting room together. . . .

The only reason why the Queen w^{ld} pause before she gives her *entire* approval of Miss Kortwright's pamphlet—is because she rather praises that *Mary Walker* who is a very objectionable woman. . . .[15]

II

For all her orthodoxy, Victoria is more than simply conventional. And her subjects know it. H.G. Wells says later:

> I do not think it is on record anywhere, but it is plain to me from what I have heard my mother say, that among school-mistresses and such like women at any rate, there was a stir of emancipation associated with the claim of the Princess Victoria . . . to succeed King William IV. There was a movement against that young lady based on her sex and this had provoked in reaction a wave of feminine partisanship throughout the country.[16]

As Queen, Victoria continues to contribute to the "stir of emancipation" which swells throughout her long reign. Not only does the monarch's very sex encourage women bent upon achievement, but Victoria herself takes an active role in liberating womankind from at least one traditional source of pain. She agrees to anesthesia during childbirth. According to Elizabeth Longford:

> In the early days of 1847 Dr Snow had written defensively: "where the pain is not greater than the patient is willing to bear cheerfully, there is no occasion to use chloroform; but when the patient is anxious to be spared the pain, I can see no valid objection to the use of this agent even in the most favourable cases." Queen

Victoria was emphatically one of "the most favourable cases", as she herself constantly boasted. Yet she was not amused at the idea of continuing to "bear cheerfully" pain which might be eliminated.[17]

Childbirth pains were traditionally considered a divinely-ordained consequence of Eve's sin. Only six years after clerics had fulminated against the first English experiments with chloroform, the English Queen in 1853 sides with womankind and defied the divine command that "in sorrow shalt thou bring forth children" (Genesis 1).

Even regarding Woman's Rights, Victoria is not entirely singleminded. She enjoys, for example, the grounds upon which a deputation of women demand the vote. "Men were seldom fit for the work."[18] Victoria's delight here is particularly important because it reflects a private attitude which runs counter to her public image—a fierce ambivalence toward the very type of man-woman relation that she experienced with Albert and helped canonize throughout her reign. Victoria is representative of her era because her sincere commitment to orthodoxy does not preclude other emotions which are in fact the stuff of the feminist arguments she excoriated.

One of these untoward emotions surfaces early in her reign. When Albert reappears at the English court in 1839 after a three-year absence, Victoria confides to her dear diary, "It was with some emotion that I beheld Albert—who is *beautiful.*"[19] The frankness of her sexual attraction is as far from the ideal of genteel prudery in her era as it is true to the facts of hetero-sexual relations in any era.

> Albert really is quite charming, and so excessively handsome . . . such beautiful blue eyes, an exquisite nose, and such a pretty mouth with delicate mustachios and slight but very slight whiskers; a beautiful figure, broad in the shoulders and a fine waist; my heart is quite going. . . . It is quite a pleasure to look at Albert when he gallops and valses, he does it so beautifully, and holds himself so well with that beautiful figure of his. . . .[20]

Especially since Victoria's marriage to this ravishing man proves so happy, her subsequent reservations about sexual relations are surprising and complicated. Writing in 1858 to just-married Vicky, Victoria touches upon various issues of the Woman Question:

Now to reply to your observation that you find a married woman had much more liberty than an unmarried one; in one sense of the word she has,—but what I meant was—in a physical point of view—and if you have hereafter (as I had constantly for the first 2 years of my marriage)—aches—and sufferings and miseries and plagues—which you must struggle against—and enjoyments etc. to give up—constant precautions to take, you will feel the yoke of a married woman! Without that—certainly it is unbounded happiness—if one has a husband one worships! It is a foretaste of heaven. And you have a husband who adores you, and is, I perceive, ready to meet every wish and desire of your's. I had 9 times for 8 months to bear with those above-named enemies and real misery (besides many duties) and I own it tried me sorely; one feels so pinned down—one's wings clipped—in fact, at the best (and few were or are better than I was) only half oneself—particularly the first and second time. This I call the "shadow side" as much as being torn away from one's loved home, parents and brothers and sisters. And therefore—I think our sex a most unenviable one.[21]

Shocking to the subjects who accepted Victoria's popular image would surely have been her attitude—here and throughout the 1858-62 letters to Vicky—toward pregnancy and babies.

I can not tell you how happy I am that you are not in an unenviable position. I never can rejoice by hearing that a poor young thing is pulled down by this trial.

Though I quite admit the comfort and blessing good and amiable children are—though they are also an awful plague and anxiety for which they show one so little gratitude very often! What made me so miserable was—to have the two first years of my married life utterly spoilt by this occupation! I could enjoy nothing—not travel about or go about with dear Papa and if I had waited a year, as I hope you will, it would have been very different. (93-94)

Besides its inconvenience, pregnancy introduces "animal" aspects which Victoria, despite her passionate nature, cannot accept unequivocally.

What you say of the pride of giving life to an immortal soul is very fine, dear, but I own I cannot enter into that; I think much more of our being like a cow or a dog at such moments; when our poor nature becomes so very animal and unecstatic. . . .

. . . I positively think those ladies who are always enceinte quite disgusting; it is more like a rabbit or guinea-pig than any-thing else and really it is not very nice. There is Lady Kildare who has two a year one in January and one in December—and always is so, whenever one sees her! And there is no end to the jokes about her! (115, 195)

Nor do the products of pregnancy please Victoria more than the process. "I hated the thought of having children and have no adoration for very little babies. . . . I am no admirer of babies generally" (167, 267). Her disaffection here had at least two sources:

> Abstractedly, I have no tendre for them till they have become a little human; an ugly baby is a very nasty object—and the prettiest is frightful when undressed—till about four months; in short as long as they have their big body and little limbs and that terrible frog-like action. But from four months, they become prettier and prettier. And I repeat it—your child would delight me at any age. (191)

Besides her evolutionary shudder here, Victoria also knows that babies could separate a woman from her husband and thus cause a tension—an orthodoxy rarely if ever acknowledged—between wife and mother.

> I know you will not forget, dear, your promise not to indulge in "baby worship", or to neglect your other greater duties in becoming a nurse.
>   . . . as my dear child is a little disorderly in regulating her time, I fear you might lose a great deal of it, if you overdid the passion for the nursery. No lady, and still less a Princess, is fit for her husband or her position, if she does that. . . . Let me repeat once more, dear, that it is very bad for any person to have them very fast—and that the poor children suffer for it, even more, not to speak of the ruin it is to the looks of a young woman—which she must not neglect for her husband's sake, particularly when she is a Princess and obliged to appear. (95-96, 143-44)

And so, without denying Victoria's great love for her children and grandchildren (especially after they had reached four months), her reservations about pregnancy and progeny echo the reservations of mothers throughout the epoch. Victoria's protest against the uncontrolled repetition of pregnancy is in-evitably shared by a largely silent multitude of dutiful Victorian women who are not "feminists" and do not want to destroy home and family. When unconventional feelings about these institutions are voiced, not by committed revolutionaries but by Queen Victoria herself, we see how far the supposed Victorian ideal diverges from Victorian life.

Another, and still more surprising, reservation appears when Victoria writes to Vicky about the conjugal relation itself.

> There is great happiness and great blessedness in devoting oneself to another who is worthy of one's affection; still men are very selfish and the woman's devotion is always one of submission which makes our poor sex so very unenviable. This you will feel hereafter—I know; though it cannot be otherwise as God has willed it so. (44)

That Victoria can add "You know, my dearest, that I never admit any other wife can be as happy as I am . . . for I maintain Papa is unlike anyone who lives or ever lived or will live" indicates how divided she and her era are.

> Men ought to have an adoration for one, and indeed to do every thing to make up, for what after all they alone are the cause of! I must say it is a bad arrangement, but we must calmly, patiently bear it, and feel that we can't help it and therefore we must forget it, and the more we retain our pure, modest feelings, the easier it is to get over it all afterwards. I am very much like a girl in all these feelings, but since I have had a grown-up married daughter, and young married relations I have been obliged to hear and talk of things and details which I hate—but which are unavoidable . . . that despising our poor degraded sex—(for what else is it as we poor creatures are born for man's pleasure and amusement, and destined to go through endless sufferings and trials?) is a little in all clever men's natures; dear Papa even is not quite exempt though he would not admit it—but he laughs and sneers constantly at many of them and at our unavoidable inconveniences, etc. though he hates the want of affection, of due attention to and protection of them, says that the men who leave all home affairs—and the education of their children to their wives—forget their first duties. (165-166, 205)

Some of Victoria's reservations partake of a quite conventional self-pity—"our poor, ill-used sex"—and others partake of an equally conventional female chauvinism. "We women are born to suffer and bear it so much more easily [than men do] . . .

woman's love exceeds what man's, I think, can ever be" (210, 310, 345). The Queen does nonetheless feel toward the institution of marriage an ambivalence which becomes increasingly characteristic of her era.

All marriage is such a lottery—the happiness is always an exchange—though it may be a very happy one—still the poor woman is bodily and morally the husband's slave. That always sticks in my throat. When I think of a merry, happy, free young girl—and look at the ailing, aching state a young wife generally is doomed to—which you can't deny is the penalty of marriage. . . .
    . . . Yes, dearest, it is an awful moment to have to give one's innocent child up to a man, be he ever so kind and good—and to think of all that she must go through! I can't say what I suffered, what I felt—what struggles I had to go through—(indeed I have not quite got over it yet) and that last night when we took you to your room, and you cried so much, I said to Papa as we came back "after all, it is like taking a poor lamb to be sacrificed". You now know—what I meant, dear. I know that God has willed it so and that these are the trials which we poor women must go through; no father, no man can feel this! Papa never would enter into it all! As in fact he seldom can in my very violent feelings. It really makes me shudder when I look around at all your sweet, happy, unconscious sisters—and think that I must give them up too—one by one!! Our dear Alice, has seen and heard more (of course not what no one ever can know before they marry and before they have had children) than you did, from your marriage—and quite enough to give her a horror rather of marrying.
    . . . Let me caution you, dear child, again, to say as little as you can on these subjects before Alice (who has already heard much more than you ever did) for she has the greatest horror of having children, and would rather have none—just as I was as a girl and when I first married—so I am very anxious she should know as little about the inevitable miseries as possible; so don't forget, dear. (254, 182, 343)

In light of her recognition of life's "shadow side," Victoria's words about Albert as "mother" become clearer. Not only is Albert far superior to the predatory bad husband, he surpasses the conventional good husband, the "protector . . . guide and adviser." Albert is "father" and even "mother." Making him into an androgynous combination of all domestic roles allows Victoria to create what she has always lacked—Home. Homemaking is, of course, the ideal of the wife-mother. And Victoria personifies that ideal for her era. But she creates Home, not by locating the domestic virtues in herself, but by positing them in Albert. Lacking every aspect of Home in her past, and recognizing the predatory potential of male passion, Victoria creates protective domesticity by creating a husband-mother. Such an androgynous ideal surfaces throughout the period and throughout these volumes—Drysdale's metaphor for human oneness, scriptural debates over the nature of the God who "created *them* in *His* image, man and woman" (Genesis 1). Role reversal in fact haunts opponents of the woman's movement. They caricature advocates of sexual equality as flat-chested women and high-voiced men, and they warn that equality would unsex both sexes. No one opposed role shifting more than the Queen (so remote was sexual inversion from her mind that the court could not discover how to inform her about lesbian love). And yet Victoria, again representative of her era, senses sufficiently the inadequacy of conventional stereotyping that she repeatedly celebrates Albert as the angel of her house. "He managed our household and home; in short, he was the life and soul of everything!"[22] In short, mother.

Recognizing the complexities of marriage and particularly its predatory aspects, Victoria finds herself praising what other Victorians for various reasons are also reexamining—the values of single life. She does not go so far as to praise celibacy or to advocate careers as an alternative to marriage, but the Queen here again expresses to Vicky feelings at variance with orthodoxy—at variance this time with the traditional belief that marriage (no matter how flaying) was woman's highest state.

> I think unmarried people are very often very happy—certainly more so than married people who don't live happily together of which there are so many instances. . . . I think people really marry far too much; it is such a lottery after all, and for a poor woman a very doubtful happiness.[23]

When Victoria refers to "my own [wedded] happiness (a happiness few if any enjoy)," her last six words are not truly parenthetical. Experience has taught her, as it did her era, that the ideal which Victoria's marriage embodied was rarely achieved in Victorian homes. The Queen thus recognizes at least some of what many contemporary writers insisted upon. That she never made public her reservations about marriage, that she stands in the succeeding years ever more staunchly against woman's rights and for the home, should not make us too critical. Like her epoch, and like us all, Victoria experiences contradictions which she cannot reconcile. When a cleric suggests with impeccable orthodoxy that Victoria consider herself the Bride of Christ after Albert's death, she replies, "That is what I call twaddle." Like all too many Victorians, the Queen can neither feel completely soothed by conventional consolations nor imagine new ones.

5

John Ruskin and "Of Queens' Gardens"

John Ruskin's "Of Queens' Gardens" (1865)[1] has been read in the twentieth century as a classic statement of the high Victorian ideal of woman.[2] The essay emphatically reaffirms a male attitude central to nineteenth-century thinking: protective devotion to the innocent girl, the angel-wife, and the home of which they are the presiding spirits. But if this were its only message, then contemporary responses to "Of Queens' Gardens" are puzzling. Although the essay was enormously popular for half a century as the articulation of an accepted cultural ideal, it was also attacked by contemporary critics as violent, "Carlylesque" social criticism. Evidently the familiar ideal could be invoked to support a social vision disturbingly different from the Victorian reality. Ruskin's praise of true womanhood became troubling when he insisted that women take responsibility for social health. In "Of Queens' Gardens" he makes more explicit the criticism of competitive materialism implicit in Sarah Lewis' *Woman's Mission.* Unlike Lewis, Ruskin appeals to women to turn that criticism into reforming action. His essay calls on the myth of the Angel in the House so often used to justify woman's radically unequal education, employment, and legal status. But here the angel is invoked not as a conservative force in a changing society, but as a potentially subversive force in the culture which imagined her. On the importance of women for realizing a "new era," Ruskin and Margaret Fuller might agree.

The point is worth exploring. Ruskin's essay on the Woman Question is indeed illuminating, but not primarily for what it says about women. He might be taken as representative of those Victorians who, for at least some period in their lives, saw the defense of women and the reform of their roles or rights as a major means of altering unsatisfactory conditions in existing society. Thompson, Tennyson, Fuller, Ruskin, and Mill had widely varying commitments to improving the status of women (Ruskin probably least of all), but each saw enlarged roles for women as a key to the reforms in which he or she was most interested. The Woman Question intersected at crucial points with the social, economic, and moral questions which the Victorians asked so persistently—and could rarely answer. "Of Queens' Gardens" is one of those intersections.

Ruskin shared the reforming zeal of Thompson, Fuller, and Mill, but not their ideas. Unlike Thompson or Mill, he did not believe in an egalitarian society. He was conservative in his estimate of women's natural ability and openly paternalistic in his treatment of them. Like Sarah Lewis in the 1830s, Ruskin in the 1860s articulated the central Victorian belief in the different natures and separate spheres of women. But Ruskin, like other high Victorian social reformers including Charles Kingsley, F.D. Maurice, and Anna Jameson, urged women to enlarge their spheres beyond the walled gardens of their own familial Edens. Women's influence, Ruskin argued, should be expanded to "queenly power"—the exercise of social responsibility outside the home. To this end, Ruskin supported improved education for women and encouraged them to concern themselves with larger social problems—helping Octavia Hill finance good low-income housing, for example. The role he envisioned for women, as most suited to their special natures, was essentially an extension of their domestic responsibilities: to be man's helpmate and moral guide, freely dispensing "order, comfort, and loveliness" to those on both sides of the garden gate. But the helpmate was also, in Ruskin's account, implicitly the critic of her spouse and his world. Her supposed natural concerns made her a powerful ally for Ruskin, perhaps the only one he could count on in the mid 1860s—for he, too, as a critic of culture and society, cared for the order, comfort, and loveliness he saw threatened in the dinary Victorian world. Ruskin's essay is as much an appeal *to* omen as an appeal *for* women—an appeal to take a more active nd, necessarily, a more openly critical role in enforcing the lues of the home in the larger world outside. This newly itical role for women, as Ruskin dramatized it in his essay, mes dangerously close to denying the true womanly ideal hich inspired it.

Ruskin himself would hardly have admitted that the tradi- onal view of woman was insufficient, for he certainly shared unquestioning, even obsessive devotion to a childlike angel- oman. The limits of his support for expanded roles for women e very evident. He was generous of his time and money to a rogressive girls' school, Winnington Hall, which offered physi- l as well as literary and artistic education at a time when few eople believed in physical exercise for girls (see illustration 4). ut the school did not, significantly, prepare women for paid bs.[3] And although he had been one of the first teachers at the Vorking Men's College in London, he was strongly opposed to e establishment of a Working Women's College.[4] Yet for all e familiar restrictiveness of Ruskin's idealizations of women, e could be, oddly, an unintentional ally of feminists, even as ey, working from other beliefs and for quite other ends, ecame his. In "Of Queens' Gardens" Ruskin has at least one oncern in common with active feminists of the high Victorian ears—the desire to get middle-class women out of their homes.

I

"Of Queens' Gardens" was originally a lecture delivered to aise money for schools in a Manchester slum. Its rhetoric eflects Ruskin's attempt to arouse middle-class men and women rom complacency to social action. The essay is organized into hree sections: a discussion of woman's nature, which includes a ostalgic picture of the pure angel presiding over the sanctuary f Home; suggestions for woman's education; and a highly olemical conclusion urging upon her much broader social re- ponsibilities. In his opening paragraphs Ruskin describes the kingly power" that had been the subject of a previous lecture. he section that follows is haunted by the presence of the girl vho embodied angelic qualities for Ruskin, Rose La Touche, with whom he was hopelessly and obsessively in love. Her image corresponds to similar figures of mothers or lost loves who continued to exercise their power over the minds of so many Victorian men and women, as they did over Tennyson's Prince and Princess (*The Princess,* 1847)—the same image of impossible purity which Sarah Lewis had urged mothers to engrave upon the hearts of their children.

> Believing that all literature and all education are only useful so far as they tend to confirm this calm, beneficent, and *therefore* kingly, power—first over ourselves, and, through ourselves, over all around us, I am now going to ask you to consider with me farther, what special portion or kind of this royal authority, arising out of noble education, may rightly be possessed by women; and how far they also are called to a true queenly power. Not in their households merely, but over all within their sphere. And in what sense, if they rightly understood and exercised this royal or gracious influence, the order and beauty induced by such benignant power would justify us in speaking of the territories over which each of them reigned, as "Queens' Gardens."
>
> And here, in the very outset, we are met by a far deeper question, which—strange though this may seem—remains among many of us yet quite undecided, in spite of its infinite importance.
>
> We cannot determine what the queenly power of women should be, until we are agreed what their ordinary power should be. We cannot consider how education may fit them for any widely extending duty, until we are agreed what is their true constant duty. And there never was a time when wilder words were spoken, or more vain imagination permitted, respecting this question— quite vital to all social happiness. The relations of the womanly to the manly nature, their different capacities of intellect or of virtue, seem never to have been yet measured with entire consent. We hear of the mission and of the rights of Woman, as if these could ever be separate from the mission and the rights of Man;—as if she and her lord were creatures of independent kind and of irreconcilable claim. This, at least, is wrong. And not less wrong—perhaps even more foolishly wrong (for I anticipate thus far what I hope to prove)—is the idea that woman is only the shadow and attendant image of her lord, owing him a thoughtless and servile obedience, and supported altogether in her weakness by the pre-eminence of his fortitude.
>
> This, I say, is the most foolish of all errors respecting her who was made to be the helpmate of man. As if he could be helped effectively by a shadow, or worthily by a slave!

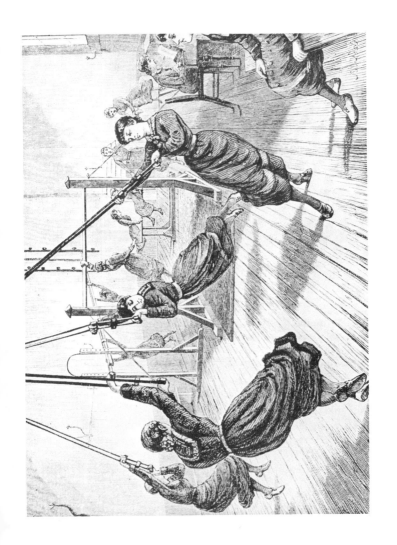

4. The Giant Stride in the Gymnasium
Girls' Own Paper, 1882

Let us try, then, whether we cannot get at some clear and harmonious idea (it must be harmonious if it is true) of what womanly mind and virtue are in power and office, with respect to man's; and how their relations, rightly accepted, aid, and increase, the vigor, and honor, and authority of both.[5]

Ruskin turns first to literature, where he finds women portrayed as "infallibly faithful and wise counsellors,—incorruptibly just and pure examples—strong always to sanctify, even when they cannot save" by the greatest writers: Shakespeare, Walter Scott, Dante, Chaucer, Spenser, Homer, and Aeschylus.

But how, you will ask, is the idea of this guiding function of the woman reconcilable with a true wifely subjection? Simply in that it is a *guiding*, not a determining, function. Let me try to show you briefly how these powers seem to be rightly distinguishable.

We are foolish, and without excuse foolish, in speaking of the "superiority" of one sex to the other, as if they could be compared in similar things. Each has what the other has not: each completes the other, and is completed by the other: they are in nothing alike, and the happiness and perfection of both depends on each asking and receiving from the other what the other only can give.

Now their separate characters are briefly these: The man's power is active, progressive, defensive. He is eminently the doer, the creator, the discoverer, the defender. His intellect is for speculation and invention: his energy for adventure, for war, and for conquest, wherever war is just, wherever conquest necessary. But the woman's power is for rule, not for battle,—and her intellect is not for invention or creation, but for sweet ordering, arrangement, and decision. She sees the qualities of things, their claims and their places. Her great function is Praise: she enters into no contest, but infallibly judges the crown of contest. By her office, and place, she is protected from all danger and temptation. The man, in his rough work in open world, must encounter all peril and trial:—to him, therefore, the failure, the offence, the inevitable error: often he must be wounded, or subdued, often misled, and *always* hardened. But he guards the woman from all this; within his house, as ruled by her, unless she herself has sought it, need enter no danger, no temptation, no cause of error or offence. This is the true nature of home—it is the place of Peace; the shelter, not only from all injury, but from all terror, doubt, and division. In so far as it is not this, it is not home; so far as the anxieties of the outer life penetrate into it, and the inconsistently-minded, unknown, unloved, or hostile society of the outer world is allowed by either husband or wife to cross the threshold, it ceases to be home; it is then only a part of that outer world which you have roofed over, and lighted fire in. But so far as it is a sacred place, a vestal temple, a temple of the hearth watched over by Household Gods, before whose faces none may come but those whom they can receive with love,—so far as it is this, and roof and fire are types only of a nobler shade and light,—shade as of the rock in a weary land, and light as of the Pharos in the stormy sea;—so far it vindicates the name, and fulfils the praise, of home.

And wherever a true wife comes, this home is always round her. The stars only may be over her head; the glow-worm in the night-cold grass may be the only fire at her foot: but home is yet wherever she is; and for a noble woman it stretches far round her, better than ceiled with cedar, or painted with vermilion, shedding its quiet light far, for those who else were homeless.

This, then, I believe to be,—will you not admit it to be,—the woman's true place and power? But do not you see that to fulfil this, she must—as far as one can use such terms of a human creature—be incapable of error? So far as she rules, all must be right, or nothing is. She must be enduringly, incorruptibly good; instinctively, infallibly wise—wise, not for self-development, but for self-renunciation: wise, not that she may set herself above her husband, but that she may never fail from his side: wise, not with the narrowness of insolent and loveless pride, but with the passionate gentleness of an infinitely variable, because infinitely applicable, modesty of service—the true changefulness of woman. In that great sense—"La donna e mobile," not "Qual piùm' al vento;" no, nor yet "Variable as the shade, by the light quivering aspen made;" but variable as the *light,* manifold in fair and serene division, that it may take the color of all that it falls upon, and exalt it. (58–60)

Ruskin's discussion of women's educational needs, in the second section of his essay, assumes that natural purity will permit woman to absorb, uncorrupted, a broader liberal education. Ruskin would protect her innocence, if necessary, through ignorance. But his proposals also have a positive goal: to develop woman's sympathetic imagination as the first step toward awakening in her a concern for the world beyond her family.

II. I have been trying, thus far, to show what should be the place, and what the power of woman. Now, secondly, we ask, What kind of education is to fit her for these?

And if you indeed think this a true conception of her office and dignity, it will not be difficult to trace the course of education which would fit her for the one, and raise her to the other.

The first of our duties to her—no thoughtful persons now doubt this,—is to secure for her such physical training and exercise as may confirm her health, and perfect her beauty: the highest refinement of that beauty being unattainable without splendor of activity and of delicate strength. To perfect her beauty, I say, and increase its power; it cannot be too powerful, nor shed its sacred light too far: only remember that all physical freedom is vain to produce beauty without a corresponding freedom of heart. There are two passages of that poet [Wordsworth] who is distinguished, it seems to me, from all others—not by power, but by exquisite *right*ness—which point you to the source, and describe to you, in a few syllables, the completion of womanly beauty. I will read the introductory stanzas, but the last is the one I wish you specially to notice:

> Three years she grew in sun and shower,
> Then Nature said, a lovelier flower
>   On earth was never sown.
> This child I to myself will take;
> She shall be mine, and I will make
>   A lady of my own.
>
> Myself will to my darling be
> Both law and impulse; and with me
>   The girl, in rock and plain,
> In earth and heaven, in glade and bower,
> Shall feel an overseeing power
>   To kindle, or restrain.
>
> The floating clouds their state shall lend
> To her, for her the willow bend;
>   Nor shall she fail to see
> Even in the motions of the storm,
> Grace that shall mould the maiden's form
>   By silent sympathy.
>
> And *vital feelings of delight*
> Shall rear her form to stately height,—
>   Her virgin bosom swell.
> Such *thoughts* to Lucy I will give,
> While she and I together live,
>   Here in this happy dell.

"*Vital* feelings of delight," observe. There are deadly feelings of delight; but the natural ones are vital, necessary to the very life. And they must be feelings of delight, if they are to be vital. Do you think you can make a girl lovely, if you do not make her happy. There is not one restraint you put on a good girl's nature—there is not one check you give to her instincts of affection or of effort—which will not be indelibly written on her features, with a hardness which is all the more painful because it takes away the brightness from the eyes of innocence, and the charm from the brow of virtue.

This for the means: now note the end. Take from the same poet, in two lines, a perfect description of womanly beauty—

A countenance in which did meet
Sweet records, promises as sweet.

The perfect loveliness of a woman's countenance can only consist in that majestic peace, which is founded in the memory of happy and useful years,—full of sweet records; and from the joining of this with that yet more majestic childishness, which is still full of change and promise;—opening always—modest at once, and bright, with hope of better things to be won, and to be bestowed. There is no old age where there is still that promise—it is eternal youth.

Thus, then, you have first to mould her physical frame, and then, as the strength she gains will permit you, to fill and temper her mind with all knowledge and thoughts which tend to confirm its natural instincts of justice, and refine its natural tact of love.

All such knowledge should be given her as may enable her to understand, and even to aid, the work of men: and yet it should be given, not as knowledge,—nor as if it were, or could be, for her an object to know; but only to feel, and to judge. It is of no moment, as a matter of pride or perfectness in herself, whether she knows many languages or one, but it is of the utmost, that she should be able to show kindness to a stranger's tongue. It is of no moment to her own worth or dignity that she should be acquainted with this science or that; but it is of the highest that she should be trained in habits of accurate thought; that she should understand the meaning, the inevitableness, and the loveliness of natural laws, and follow at least some one path of scientific attainment, as far as to the threshold of that bitter Valley of Humiliation, into which only the wisest and bravest of men can descend, owning themselves forever children, gathering pebbles on a boundless shore. It is of little consequence how many positions of cities she knows, or how many dates of events, or how many names of celebrated persons—

it is not the object of education to turn a woman into a dictionary; but it is deeply necessary that she should be taught to enter with her whole personality into the history she reads; to picture the passages of it vitally in her own bright imagination; to apprehend, with her fine instincts, the pathetic circumstances and dramatic relations, which the historian too often only eclipses by his reasoning, and disconnects by his arrangement: it is for her to trace the hidden equities of divine reward, and catch sight, through the darkness, of the fateful threads of woven fire that connect error with its retribution. But, chiefly of all, she is to be taught to extend the limits of her sympathy with respect to that history which is being forever determined, as the moments pass in which she draws her peaceful breath; and to the contemporary calamity which, were it but rightly mourned by her, would recur no more hereafter. She is to exercise herself in imagining what would be the effects upon her mind and conduct, if she were daily brought into the presence of the suffering which is not the less real because shut from her sight. She is to be taught somewhat to understand the nothingness of the proportion which that little world in which she lives and loves, bears to the world in which God lives and loves;—and solemnly she is to be taught to strive that her thoughts of piety may not be feeble in proportion to the number they embrace, nor her prayer more languid than it is for the momentary relief from pain of her husband or her child, when it is uttered for the multitudes of those who have none to love them,—and is "for all who are desolate and oppressed."

Thus far, I think, I have had your concurrence, perhaps you will not be with me in what I believe is most needful for me to say. There *is* one dangerous science for women—one which let them indeed beware how they profanely touch—that of theology. Strange, and miserably strange, that while they are modest enough to doubt their powers, and pause at the threshold of sciences where every step is demonstrable and sure, they will plunge headlong, and without one thought of incompetency, into that science in which the greatest men have trembled, and the wisest erred. Strange, that they will complacently and pridefully bind up whatever vice or folly there is in them, whatever arrogance, petulance, or blind incomprehensiveness, into one bitter bundle of consecrated myrrh. Strange, in creatures born to be Love visible, that where they can know least they will condemn first, and think to recommend themselves to their Master by scrambling up the steps of His judgment throne, to divide it with Him. Most strange, that they should think they were led by the Spirit of the Comforter into habits of mind which have become in them the unmixed elements of home discomfort; and that they dare to turn the Household

Gods of Christianity into ugly idols of their own—spiritual dolls, for them to dress according to their caprice: and from which their husbands must turn away in grieved contempt, lest they should be shrieked at for breaking them.

I believe, then, with this exception, that a girl's education should be nearly, in its course and material of study, the same as a boy's, but quite differently directed. A woman, in any rank of life, ought to know whatever her husband is likely to know, but to know it in a different way. His command of it should be foundational and progressive, hers, general and accomplished for daily and helpful use. Not but that it would often be wiser in men to learn things in a womanly sort of way, for present use, and to seek for the discipline and training of their mental powers in such branches of study as will be afterwards fittest for social service; but, speaking broadly, a man ought to know any language or science he learns, thoroughly, while a woman ought to know the same language, or science, only so far as may enable her to sympathize in her husband's pleasures, and in those of his best friends.

Yet, observe, with exquisite accuracy as far as she reaches. There is a wide difference between elementary knowledge and superficial knowledge—between a firm beginning, and a feeble smattering. A woman may always help her husband by what she knows, however little; by what she half-knows, or mis-knows, she will only tease him.

And, indeed, if there were to be any difference between a girl's education and a boy's, I should say that of the two the girl's should be earlier led, as her intellect ripens faster, into deep and serious subjects; and that her range of literature should be, not more, but less frivolous, calculated to add the qualities of patience and seriousness to her natural poignancy of thought and quickness of wit; and also to keep her in a lofty and pure element of thought. I enter not now into any question of choice of books; only be sure that her books are not heaped up in her lap as they fall out of the package of the circulating library, wet with the last and lightest spray of the fountain of folly.

. . . And if she can have access to a good library of old and classical books, there need be no choosing at all. Keep the modern magazine and novel out of your girl's way: turn her loose into the old library every wet day, and let her alone. She will find what is good for her; you cannot: for there is just this difference between the making of a girl's character and a boy's—you may chisel a boy into shape, as you would a rock, or hammer him into it, if he be of a better kind, as you would a piece of bronze. But you cannot hammer a girl into anything. She grows as a flower does,—she will wither without sun; she will decay in her sheath as the narcissus does, if you do not give her air enough; she may fall, and defile her head in dust, if you leave her without help at some moments of her life; but you cannot fetter her; she must take her own fair form and way, if she take any, and in mind as in body must have always

> Her household motions light and free
> And steps of virgin liberty.

Let her loose in the library, I say, as you do a fawn in a field. It knows the bad weeds twenty times better than you; and the good ones too, and will eat some bitter and prickly ones, good for it, which you had not the slightest thought were good.

Then, in art, keep the finest models before her, and let her practice in all accomplishments be accurate and thorough, so as to enable her to understand more than she accomplishes. I say the finest models—that is to say, the truest, simplest, usefullest. Note those epithets; they will range through all the arts. Try them in music, there you might think them the least applicable. I say the truest, that in which the notes most closely and faithfully express the meaning of the words, or the character of intended emotion; again, the simplest, that in which the meaning and melody are attained with the fewest and most significant notes possible; and, finally, the usefullest, that music which makes the best words most beautiful, which enchants them in our memories each with its own glory of sound, and which applies them closest to the heart at the moment we need them.

And not only in the material and in the course, but yet more earnestly in the spirit of it, let a girl's education be as serious as a boy's. You bring up your girls as if they were meant for sideboard ornaments, and then complain of their frivolity. Give them the same advantages that you give their brothers—appeal to the same grand instincts of virtue in them; teach *them* also that courage and truth are the pillars of their being: do you think that they would not answer that appeal, brave and true as they are even now, when you know that there is hardly a girl's school in this Christian kingdom where the children's courage or sincerity would be thought of half so much importance as their way of coming in at a door; and when the whole system of society, as respects the mode of establishing them in life, is one rotten plague of cowardice and imposture,—cowardice, in not daring to let them live, or love, except as their neighbors choose; and imposture, in bringing, for the purpose of our own pride, the full glow of the world's worst vanity upon a girl's eyes, at the very period when the whole happiness of her future existence depends upon her remaining undazzled?

And give them, lastly, not only noble teachings, but noble teachers. You consider somewhat, before you send your boy to school, what kind of a man the master is;—whatsoever kind of man he is, you at least give him full authority over your son, and show some respect to him yourself; if he comes to dine with you, you do not put him at a side table; you know also that, at his college, your child's immediate tutor will be under the direction of some still higher tutor, for whom you have absolute reverence. You do not treat the Dean of Christ Church or the Master of Trinity as your inferiors.

But what teachers do you give your girls, and what reverence do you show to the teachers you have chosen? Is a girl likely to think her own conduct, or her own intellect, of much importance, when you trust the entire formation of her character, moral and intellectual, to a person whom you let your servants treat with less respect than they do your housekeeper (as if the soul of your child were a less charge than jams and groceries), and whom you yourself think you confer an honor upon by letting her sometimes sit in the drawing-room in the evening?

Thus, then, of literature as her help, and thus of art. There is one more help which she cannot do without—one which, alone, has sometimes done more than all other influences besides,—the help of wild and fair nature. . . .

Now, you cannot, indeed, have here in England, woods eighteen miles deep to the centre; but you can, perhaps, keep a fairy or two for your children yet, if you wish to keep them. But *do* you wish it? Suppose you had each, at the back of your houses, a garden, large enough for your children to play in, with just as much lawn as would give them room to run,—no more—and that you could not change your abode; but that, if you choose, you could double your income, or quadruple it, by digging a coal shaft in the middle of the lawn, and turning the flower-beds into heaps of coke. Would you do it? I think not. I can tell you, you would be wrong if you did, though it gave you income sixty-fold instead of four-fold.

Yet this is what you are doing with all England. The whole country is but a little garden, not more than enough for your children to run on the lawns of, if you would let them *all* run there. And this little garden you will turn into furnace-ground, and fill with heaps of cinders, if you can; and those children of yours, not you, will suffer for it. For the fairies will not be all banished; there are fairies of the furnace as of the wood, and their first gifts seem to be "sharp arrows of the mighty;" but their last gifts are "coals of juniper."

And yet I cannot—though there is no part of my subject that I feel more—press this upon you; for we made so little use of the power of nature while we had it that we shall hardly feel what we have lost. Just on the other side of the Mersey you have your Snowdon, and your Menai Straits, and that mighty granite rock beyond the moors of Anglesea, splendid in its heathery crest, and foot planted in the deep sea, once thought of as sacred—a divine promontory, looking westward; the Holy Head or Headland, still not without awe when its red light glares first through storm. These are the hills, and these the bays and blue inlets, which, among the Greeks, would have been always loved, always fateful in influence on the national mind. That Snowdon is your Parnassus; but where are its Muses? That Holyhead mountain is your Island of AEgina, but where is its temple to Minerva?

Shall I read you what the Christian Minerva had achieved under the shadow of our Parnassus, up to the year 1848?—Here is a little account of a Welsh school, from page 261 of the Report on Wales, published by the Committee of Council on Education. This is a school close to a town containing 5000 persons:—

> I then called up a larger class, most of whom had recently come to the school. Three girls repeatedly declared they had never heard of Christ, and two that they had never heard of God. Two out of six thought Christ was on earth now ("they might have had a worse thought, perhaps"), three knew nothing about the crucifixion. Four out of seven did not know the names of the months, nor the number of days in a year. They had no notion of addition beyond two and two, or three and three; their minds were perfect blanks.

O ye women of England! from the Princess of that Wales to the simplest of you, do not think your own children can be brought into their true fold of rest while these are scattered on the hills, as sheep having no shepherd. And do not think your daughters can be trained to the truth of their own human beauty, while the pleasant places, which God made at once for their school-room and their play-ground, lie desolate and defiled. You cannot baptize them rightly in those inch-deep fonts of yours, unless you baptize them also in the sweet waters which the great Lawgiver strikes forth forever from the rocks of your native land—waters which a Pagan would have worshipped in their purity, and you only worship with pollution. You cannot lead your children faithfully to those narrow axe-hewn church altars of yours, while the dark azure altars in heaven—the mountains that sustain your island throne, —mountains on which a Pagan would have seen the powers of heaven rest in every wreathed cloud—remain for you without inscription; altars built, not to, but by, an Unknown God. (60-71)

In the last section of his essay, Ruskin's tone changes dramatically. No longer evoking an ideal of protected innocence, or counseling middle-class parents on the education of daughters, he turns on the women in his audience and accuses them of a criminal apathy and indifference. The nostalgic vision of the naturally pure woman fades in the face of a different reality: bloody fields, dismal coal heaps, and the dark, terrible streets of Manchester into which, Ruskin cries, woman must now enter. He no longer insists on the necessary innocence-in-ignorance of his queens. They must concern themselves not only with flowers but with "feeble florets": the impoverished, the ill-educated, and the economically oppressed—including, as Fuller too had insisted, prostitutes. As she leaves her garden for an active life in the world, the angelic Lucy of Ruskin's first section becomes the Maud and Magdalen of his last—a woman whose sympathy is born not of natural innocence but of passionate knowledge.[6] Logically, the first and last sections, Ruskin's praise of woman's ordinary nature within the home and his demand for queenly action outside it, involve contradictions which he never resolves. But structurally and rhetorically, despite his evocation of the angelic ideal, Ruskin clearly emphasizes the last section: his attempt to get comfortable middle-class women to leave their park walls and garden gates for a world of wilderness and secrets and suffering.

III. Thus far, then, of the nature, thus far of the teaching, of woman, and thus of her household office, and queenliness. We come now to our last, our widest question,—What is her queenly office with respect to the state?

Generally, we are under an impression that a man's duties are public, and a woman's private. But this is not altogether so. A man has a personal work or duty, relating to his own home, and a public work or duty, which is the expansion of the other, relating to the state. So a woman has a personal work or duty, relating to her own home, and a public work and duty, which is also the expansion of that.

Now the man's work for his own home is, as has been said, to secure its maintenance, progress, and defence; the woman's to secure its order, comfort, and loveliness.

Expand both these functions. The man's duty as a member of a commonwealth is to assist in the maintenance, in the advance, in the defence of the state. The woman's duty, as a member of the commonwealth, is to assist in the ordering, in the comforting, and in the beautiful adornment of the state.

What the man is at his own gate, defending it, if need be, against insult and spoil, that also, not in a less, but in a more devoted measure, he is to be at the gate of his country, leaving his home, if need be, even to the spoiler, to do his more incumbent work there.

And, in like manner, what the woman is to be within her gates, as the centre of order, the balm of distress, and the mirror of beauty; that she is also to be without her gates, where order is more difficult, distress more imminent, loveliness more rare.

And as within the human heart there is always set an instinct for all its real duties,—an instinct which you cannot quench, but only warp and corrupt if you withdraw it from its true purpose;—as there is the intense instinct of love, which, rightly disciplined, maintains all the sanctities of life, and, misdirected, undermines them; and *must* do either the one or the other; so there is in the human heart an inextinguishable instinct, the love of power, which, rightly directed, maintains all the majesty of law and life, and misdirected, wrecks them.

Deep rooted in the innermost life of the heart of man, and of the heart of woman, God set it there, and God keeps it there. Vainly, as falsely, you blame or rebuke the desire of power!—For Heaven's sake, and for Man's sake, desire it all you can. But *what* power? That is all the question. Power to destroy? the lion's limb, and the dragon's breath? Not so. Power to heal, to redeem, to guide and to guard. Power of the sceptre and shield; the power of the royal hand that heals in touching,—that binds the fiend and looses the captive; the throne that is founded on the rock of Justice, and descended from only by steps of mercy. Will you not covet such power as this, and seek such throne as this, and be no more housewives, but queens?

It is now long since the women of England arrogated, universally, a title which once belonged to nobility only; and, having once been in the habit of accepting the simple title of gentlewoman, as correspondent to that of gentleman, insisted on the privilege of assuming the title of "Lady,"* which properly corresponds only to the title of "Lord."

I do not blame them for this; but only for their narrow motive in this. I would have them desire and claim the title of Lady,

---

*I wish there were a true order of chivalry instituted for our English youth of certain ranks, in which both boy and girl should receive, at a given age, their knighthood and ladyhood by true title; attainable only by certain probation and trial both of character and accomplishment; and to be forfeited, on conviction, by their peers, of any dishonorable act. Such an institution would be entirely, and with all noble results, possible, in a nation which loved honor. That it would not be possible among us, is not to the discredit of the scheme.

provided they claim, not merely the title, but the office and duty signified by it. Lady means "bread-giver" or "loaf-giver," and Lord means "maintainer of laws;" and both titles have reference, not to the law which is maintained in the house, nor to the bread which is given to the household; but to law maintained for the multitude, and to bread broken among the multitude. So that a Lord has legal claim only to his title in so far as he is the maintainer of the justice of the Lord of Lords; and a Lady has legal claim to her title, only so far as she communicates that help to the poor representatives of her Master, which women once, ministering to Him of their substance, were permitted to extend to that Master Himself; and when she is known, as He Himself once was, in breaking of bread.

And this beneficent and legal dominion, this power of the Dominus, or House Lord, and of the Domina or House-Lady, is great and venerable, not in the number of those through whom it has lineally descended, but in the number of those whom it grasps within its sway; it is always regarded with reverent worship where ever its dynasty is founded on its duty, and its ambition co-relative with its beneficence. Your fancy is pleased with the thought of being noble ladies, with a train of vassals. Be it so; you cannot be too noble, and your train cannot be too great; but see to it that your train is of vassals whom you serve and feed, not merely of slaves who serve and feed *you;* and that the multitude which obeys you is of those whom you have comforted, not oppressed,—whom you have redeemed, not led into captivity.

And this, which is true of the lower or household dominion, is equally true of the queenly dominion;—that highest dignity is open to you, if you will also accept that highest duty. Rex et Regina—Roi et Reine—"*Right*-doers;" they differ but from the Lady and Lord, in that their power is supreme over the mind as over the person—that they not only feed and clothe, but direct and teach. And whether consciously or not, you must be, in many a heart, enthroned: there is no putting by that crown; queens you must always be; queens to your lovers; queens to your husbands and your sons; queens of higher mystery to the world beyond, which bows itself, and will forever bow, before the myrtle crown, and the stainless sceptre, of womanhood. But, alas! you are too often idle and careless queens, grasping at majesty in the least things, while you abdicate it in the greatest; and leaving misrule and violence to work their will among men, in defiance of the power, which, holding straight in gift from the Prince of all Peace, the wicked among you betray, and the good forget.

"Prince of Peace." Note that name. When kings rule in that name, and nobles, and the judges of the earth, they also, in their narrow place, and mortal measure, receive the power of it. There are no other rulers than they: other rule than theirs is but *mis*rule;

they who govern verily "Dei gratiâ" are all princes, yes, or princesses, of peace. There is not a war in the world, no, nor an injustice, but you women are answerable for it; not in that you have provoked, but in that you have not hindered. Men, by their nature, are prone to fight; they will fight for any cause, or for none. It is for you to choose their cause for them, and to forbid them when there is no cause. There is no suffering, no injustice, no misery in the earth, but the guilt of it lies lastly with you. Men can bear the sight of it, but you should not be able to bear it. Men may tread it down without sympathy in their own struggle; but men are feeble in sympathy, and contracted in hope; it is you only who can feel the depths of pain; and conceive the way of its healing. Instead of trying to do this, you turn away from it; you shut yourselves within your park walls and garden gates; and you are content to know that there is beyond them a whole world in wilderness—a world of secrets which you dare not penetrate; and of suffering which you dare not conceive.

I tell you that this is to me quite the most amazing among the phenomena of humanity. I am surprised at no depths to which, when once warped from its honor, that humanity can be degraded. I do not wonder at the miser's death, with his hands, as they relax, dropping gold. I do not wonder at the sensualist's life, with the shroud wrapped about his feet. I do not wonder at the single-handed murder of a single victim, done by the assassin in the darkness of the railway, or reed-shadow of the marsh. I do not even wonder at the myriad-handed murder of multitudes, done boastfully in the daylight, by the frenzy of nations, and the immeasurable, unimaginable guilt, heaped up from hell to heaven, of their priests, and kings. But this is wonderful to me—oh, how wonderful!—to see the tender and delicate woman among you, with her child at her breast, and a power, if she would wield it, over it, and over its father, purer than the air of heaven, and stronger than the seas of the earth—nay, a magnitude of blessing which her husband would not part with for all that earth itself, though it were made of one entire and perfect chrysolite:—to see her abdicate this majesty to play at precedence with her next-door neighbor! This is wonderful—oh, wonderful!—to see her, with every innocent feeling fresh within her, go out in the morning into her garden to play with the fringes of its guarded flowers, and lift their heads when they are drooping, with her happy smile upon her face, and no cloud upon her brow, because there is a little wall around her place of peace: and yet she knows, in her heart, if she would only look for its knowledge, that, outside of that little rose-covered wall, the wild grass, to the horizon, is torn up by the agony of men, and beat level by the drift of their life-blood.

Have you ever considered what a deep under meaning there

lies, or at least, may be read, if we choose, in our custom of strewing flowers before those whom we think most happy? Do you suppose it is merely to deceive them into the hope that happiness is always to fall thus in showers at their feet?—that wherever they pass they will tread on herbs of sweet scent, and that the rough ground will be made smooth for them by depth of roses? So surely as they believe that, they will have, instead, to walk on bitter herbs and thorns; and the only softness to their feet will be of snow. But it is not thus intended they should believe: there is a better meaning in that old custom. The path of a good woman is indeed strewn with flowers; but they rise behind her steps, not before them. "Her feet have touched the meadows, and left the daisies rosy." You think that only a lover's fancy;—false and vain! How if it could be true? You think this also, perhaps, only a poet's fancy—

> Even the light harebell raised its head
> Elastic from her airy tread.

But it is little to say of a woman, that she only does not destroy where she passes. She should revive; the harebells should bloom, not stoop, as she passes. You think I am going into wild hyperbole? Pardon me, not a whit—I mean what I say in calm English, spoken in resolute truth. You have heard it said—(and I believe there is more than fancy even in that saying, but let it pass for a fanciful one)—that flowers only flourish rightly in the garden of some one who loves them. I know you would like that to be true; you would think it a pleasant magic if you could flush your flowers into brighter bloom by a kind look upon them: nay, more, if your look had the power, not only to cheer, but to guard them—if you could bid the black blight turn away, and the knotted caterpillar spare— if you could bid the dew fall upon them in the drought, and say to the south wind, in frost—"Come, thou south, and breathe upon my garden, that the spices of it may flow out." This you would think a great thing? And do you think it not a greater thing, that all this, (and how much more than this!) you *can* do, for fairer flowers than these—flowers that could bless you for having blessed them, and will love you for having loved them;—flowers that have eyes like yours, and thoughts like yours, and lives like yours; which, once saved, you save forever? Is this only a little power? Far among the moorlands and the rocks,—far in the darkness of the terrible streets,—these feeble florets are lying, with all their fresh leaves torn, and their stems broken—will you never go down to them, nor set them in order in their little fragrant beds, nor fence them in their shuddering from the fierce wind? Shall morning follow morning, for you, but not for them; and the dawn rise to watch, far away, those frantic Dances of Death; but no dawn rise to breathe upon these living banks of wild violet, and woodbine, and rose; nor call to you, through your casement,—call, (not giving you the name of the English poet's [Tennyson's] lady, but the name of Dante's great Matilda, who, on the edge of happy Lethe, stood, wreathing flowers with flowers,) saying:—

> Come into the garden, Maud,
> For the black bat, night, has flown;
> And the woodbine spices are wafted abroad
> And the musk of the roses blown?

Will you not go down among them?—among those sweet living things, whose new courage, sprung from the earth with the deep color of heaven upon it, is starting up in strength of goodly spire; and whose purity, washed from the dust, is opening, bud by bud, into the flower of promise;—and still they turn to you, and for you, "The Larkspur listens—I hear, I hear! And the Lily whispers—I wait."

Did you notice that I missed two lines when I read you that first stanza: and think that I had forgotten them? Hear them now:—

> Come into the garden, Maud,
> For the black bat, night, has flown;
> Come into the garden, Maud,
> I am here at the gate, alone.

Who is it, think you, who stands at the gate of this sweeter garden, alone, waiting for you? Did you ever hear, not of a Maude, but a Madeleine, who went down to her garden in the dawn, and found One waiting at the gate, whom she supposed to be the gardener? Have you not sought Him often;—sought Him in vain, all through the night;—sought Him in vain at the gate of that old garden where the fiery sword is set? He is never there; but at the gate of *this* garden He is waiting always—waiting to take your hand—ready to go down to see the fruits of the valley, to see whether the vine has flourished, and the pomegranate budded. There you shall see with Him the little tendrils of the vines that His hand is guiding—there you shall see the pomegranate springing where His hand cast the sanguine seed;—more: you shall see the troops of the angel keepers that, with their wings, wave away the hungry birds from the pathsides where He has sown, and call to each other between the vineyard rows, "Take us the foxes, the little foxes, that spoil the vines, for our vines have tender grapes." Oh—you queens—you queens; among the hills and happy greenwood of this land of yours, shall the foxes have holes, and the birds of the air have nests; and, in your cities, shall the stones cry out against you, that they are the only pillows where the Son of Man can lay His head? (71-79)

II

The argument for some extension of woman's sphere was neither new nor controversial by the 1860s. Ruskin's essay did not evoke anything like the debate over Mill's *The Subjection of Women* four years later. Sales indicate that it was widely read. *Sesame and Lilies*, the volume that contained "Of Queens' Gardens" and "Of Kings' Treasuries," had gone through eight editions by 1882, as many as the first volume of Ruskin's best-known work, *Modern Painters*. In America, where the *Critic* in 1898 called Ruskin one of the four most famous living authors (together with Twain, Tolstoi, and Zola), *Sesame and Lilies* was his most popular book. It was reprinted more than thirty-five times in the nineteenth century. In the early 1900s it was still a popular high school text.[7] An article in the *North American Review* of 1866 suggests the grounds for this lasting popularity.

> This preacher of "women's rights" differs from others in this, that the others wish women to take up some part of man's duty, and to fill some part at least of his place. Disguised under what form soever it may be of real philanthropy and earnest desire to reform crying evils, it is the tendency of most discussion of woman's sphere and mission to seek an answer to this question,—"How much of men's work ought women to do?" But the true question, thinks Mr. Ruskin, is this: "What is women's own work which men cannot do?" And the duty of man toward woman is, not to invite her to work with him at tasks which she is not fitted to undertake, but to help her to the true understanding of her own duties, and to respect and reverence her in her proper discharge of those duties.[8]

Although "Of Queens' Gardens" was appreciated by educators and the general public, it was perceived by many contemporary critics as an angry attack on traditional values. The conservative *Blackwood's* spoke of Ruskin's "extravagant charges and impossible remedies" and called *Sesame and Lilies* a "clever farrago of unmitigated abuse to the one sex, and of sugared abuse and railing flattery, of ill usage and petting, to the other."[9]

The *Saturday Review* accused him of "ungovernable spleen" and compared his words to "the shriekings of the revivalist."[10] Ruskin had made his reputation in the 1840s and 1850s as the most eloquent art critic England had ever known, but in the 1860s he became an outspoken social critic, lambasting laissez-faire economics and attacking the misery and materialism of the new industrial society. Many of the critics who disliked his new book saw it as more unwanted meddling by a man who ought to keep to art. Ruskin's "desire to preach sermons instead of making music" provoked Anthony Trollope to comment in the *Fortnightly*:

> Mr. Ruskin is well known to us as an art-critic, and as one who has written to us on Art in language so beautiful, and with words so powerful, that he has carried men and women away with him in crowds, even before he has convinced their judgments or made intelligible to them the laws which he has inculcated. He has been as the fiddler in the tale, who, when he fiddled, made all men and women dance, even though they were men and women by nature very little given to such exercise. But the fiddler was thus powerful because he understood the art of fiddling. Had he dropped his bow, and got into a pulpit that he might preach, we may doubt whether by his preaching he would have held the crowds whom his music had collected. To a fiddler so foolishly ambitious, *Ne sutor ultra crepidam* would have been the advice given by all his friends. It seems that the same advice is needed in this case. Mr. Ruskin had become a musician very potent,—powerful to charm as well as to teach. We danced, and were delighted that we could dance to such music. But now he has become ashamed of his violin, and tells us that his old skill was a thing of nought. He will leave talking to us of the beauties of art and nature, of the stones of Venice and the wild flowers of Switzerland, and will preach to us out of a high pulpit on political economy and the degradation of men and the duties of women! . . . it is much to be hoped that he will return to that work which he can do better than any of his compeers.[11]

But the radical *Westminster Review* applauded Ruskin's diatribe: "the tone of its feeling [is] pitched often far too high, and most difficult to be understood by a certain class of minds; and yet . . . [it is] not at all difficult to be understood by those who have suffered from the flippancy and hardness of the day." "Utopianism is at times good for us," the reviewer went on, "if it be only to lift us out of our usual atmosphere of prudence and pence."[12] Contemporary reviews, both critical and favorable, reacted most strongly to precisely the element of Ruskin's book that it is easy to overlook today: its character as fierce, accusatory social criticism, directed not only against social conditions in Manchester or rural Wales, but implicitly against the middle classes, where women were taught *not* to concern themselves with the world outside the home.

Most reviewers read "Of Queens' Gardens" as a continuation of the first lecture in *Sesame and Lilies.* At the close of that lecture, "Of Kings' Treasuries," Ruskin had turned from his discussion of the importance of good books to confront his middle-class audience with the same bitter accusations of apathy he was later to direct against women.

> No reading is possible for a people with its mind in this state. . . . It is simply and sternly impossible for the English public, at this moment, to understand any thoughtful writing,—so incapable of thought has it become in its insanity of avarice. . . . No nation can last, which has made a mob of itself, however generous at heart. . . . Above all, a nation cannot last as a money-making mob: it cannot with impunity,—it cannot with existence,—go on despising literature, despising science, despising art, despising nature, despising compassion, and concentrating its soul on Pence. Do you think these are harsh or wild words? . . . I will prove their truth to you, clause by clause.[13]

Contemporary critics did not miss the conscious parallels of tone and message between the two lectures. As Ruskin had intended, they heard both lectures as an attack on middle-class values, urging men and women out of their accustomed roles into new areas of social responsibility and power.

The most extended favorable review which *Sesame and Lilies* received appeared in *Victoria Magazine*, a periodical written and published by women at the center of the movement for better education and more jobs. The first part of the article takes issue, however, with the limitations Ruskin places on women's education. (The *Saturday Review*, quick to seize on an absurdity, had already made fun of Ruskin's stipulation that knowledge "should be given, not as knowledge—not as if it were or could be for her an object to know; but only to feel and judge." How, they demanded," can a woman be said to *feel* Concomitant Variations?"[14]) The *Victoria* reviewer questioned both Ruskin's assumption that women do not need to work and his belief that girls should be educated for the sake of their husbands' talents.

But after we drink in with thirsty ear this spirit-stirring draught, and though our hearts swell with gratitude towards the man who can thus nobly conceive and trace out woman's mission, we still feel that the one great urgent question of the day in regard to woman he has left untouched. It is the burden of an old song he sings to us, though in more exalted strain; but there is a song of the present day—the "Song of the Shirt"—which still keeps sounding on our ear, reminding us that woman has to work, not only in queens' gardens, but in the busy mart, and for the coarse bread of life; that she is not only the helpmate of man—the dispenser of all that is loveliest in home—but that she has often, alone and unsupported, to live without a home to sweeten, and wander forth in the rough and stony places of the world's highway. . . . we think Mr. Ruskin has overlooked the fact, that while there is a surplus of at least half a million of women, it is worse than useless, in offering suggestions upon education, to propound the theory that a woman is to be educated "only so far as may enable her to sympathise in her husband's pleasures, and in those of his best friends."

But let us put the first difficulty on one side, and suppose that the girl does marry. In obedience to the instructions Mr. Ruskin gives in another place, having shown very early a bias towards botany, she has acquired the elementary knowledge of it with "exquisite accuracy;" but how will his theory work if she marries a Max Müller, who might only care for languages, which she has never studied? Would Mr. Ruskin have wished Madame de Staël's intellectual power to have only enabled her to sympathise in her husband's pleasures? The mental companionship which is improving, is communion between active minds, and the highest purposes of marriage are unfulfilled if either husband or wife live in a region of thought the other cannot enter. We cannot but take exception to what verges on Milton's theory. . . .

It is very strange to see what impossible beings almost all men make their ideal women. They may be very charming, but they are not human. Girls are to be highly educated, and their minds fully cultivated, in order to make them meet companions for the lords of creation; and yet (we suppose to preserve that "bloom" which we hear so much about, and which appears to be something men invariably regret when speaking of a woman who has ceased to be vacant and frivolous) their minds are to stop short at certain points, and to present a perfect vacancy on some subjects, in spite of the fact that when a mind is once thoroughly awakened and active, everything which comes before it must be thought about and judged. It is more logical to state at once a preference for the bright sweet-tempered woman, whose spirits have never for a moment been checked by a puzzling thought since her school-room days and who doubtless spreads a brighter illusion on all things at home and abroad, but who, on intellectual subjects, is no companion to her husband or anyone else—than for the educated cultured woman, who as such, must naturally have her own thoughts on all important subjects.

There is a splendid passage in Mr. Ruskin's "Stones of Venice" [1852–53] upon education, which is, to our minds, applicable to both sexes alike. We shall quote the passage at length, for we think the education there described comes nearer to the requirements of women than the suggestions offered in his "Queens' Gardens."

"Education is the leading human souls to what is best, and making what is best out of them; and these two objects are always attainable together, and by the same means; the training which makes men happiest in themselves, also makes them most service-able to others. True education then has respect—first, to the ends which are proposable to the man, or attainable by him; and, secondly, to the material he is made of. So far as it is able, it chooses the *end* according to the *material*; but it cannot always choose the end, for the position of many persons in life is fixed by necessity; still less can it choose the material; and therefore all it can do is to fit the one to the other, as wisely as may be. But the first point to be understood is, that the *material* is as various as the *ends*; that not only one man is unlike another, but every man is essentially different from every other; so that no training, no forming, nor informing, will ever make two persons alike in thought or in power. Among all men, whether of the upper or lower orders, the differences are eternal and irreconcilable, be-tween one individual and another, born under absolutely the same circumstances."[15]

With the crucial third section of Ruskin's lecture, however, the *Victoria* critic agreed completely. The article continues with a discussion of woman's power that reiterates Ruskin's position—the need to extend woman's sympathies outside the home.

That the love of power should be rightly directed in women is most important for the interests of humanity. The principle is there—direct it aright, and you have women exercising the wise and beneficent influence of an Isabella of Castile; ignore it, and it will assert itself in the baneful form of a Catherine de Medici.

The thirst for power is the root of that spirit of flirtation which is so rife in the present day, and which has called forth from many of our leading papers such severe but just strictures upon women. But it is of no use to condemn without providing the remedy, and people have been too ready to stigmatise the love of power as altogether mischievous, regardless of the fact that it is an "inextinguishable instinct," only waiting for a right direction to be a mighty engine for good.

That a woman should influence her husband, few dispute, and many regard it as her only legitimate sphere of action. Whatever theory may be entertained, it is certain that wives will exercise this influence, and therefore it is essential that the influence should be of the right kind. It is melancholy to find how seldom it is exerted on the side of public virtue, and how often it discourages an effort of principle, by which the private interests, or worldly vanities, of the family may suffer. A sense of duty towards the public good, as a woman is now educated, is rarely found in her, and when we compare the wife's power with the use she makes of it, we do not wonder at Mr. Ruskin's amazement at seeing her "abdicate this majesty to play at precedence with her next door neighbour;" and we are forced to own that the picture drawn of her indifference to the misery beyond her own "rose-covered wall" is not an exaggerated one, and that for the most part instead of "feeling the depths of pain, and conceiving the way of its healing," she turns away from it, and shuts herself up within her own park walls and garden gates, content to know that there is beyond them a whole world in wilderness—a world of secrets which she dares not penetrate, and of suffering which she dares not conceive.

But before we aim at making the spirit of woman more powerful in the affairs of the world, according to its gifts and its own specialties, even to the full measure of its capacities, we must educate her in questions of public and national morality, in the fulfilment of public duty, and teach her to take an active, healthful interest in all which appertains to human life and destiny.

We have pointed out one or two matters on which we have felt ourselves at issue with Mr. Ruskin, but we cannot conclude without expressing our gratitude for this valuable contribution towards the solution of that difficult question—how to turn the powers of women to the best and highest advantage? . . . to those who feel with him, his words strike home with the power of revelation.[16]

Beside this laudatory notice from feminists, however, one must put Mill's sober comment on "queenly power": ". . . neither in the affairs of families nor in those of states is power a compensation for the loss of freedom."[17] *The Subjection of Women,* largely written by 1862 though not published until 1869, is probably not a direct reply to Ruskin. But this very different vision of both a reformed society and women's role in it requires that Mill, like Thompson before him, deny completely the grounds of Ruskin's appeal.

> The love of power and the love of liberty are in eternal antagonism. Where there is least liberty, the passion for power is the most ardent and unscrupulous. The desire of power over others can only cease to be a depraving agency among mankind, when each of them individually is able to do without it: which can only be where respect for liberty in the personal concerns of each is an established principle.[18]

Freedom and equality, on the one hand; on the other, power and responsibility in the service of order, comfort, and loveliness. To both these opposing conceptions of a better life the position of women was viewed by Victorians as crucial.

6

Eliza Lynn Linton and "The Girl of the Period"

Eliza Lynn Linton sparked one of the great Victorian controversies when she wrote "The Girl of the Period" in 1868. Important for this alone, Linton is also a synthetic figure of the period. She, like so many contemporaries, suffers the dislocating shock of a crisis of religious faith; and she, like her Queen, struggles to reconcile impulses and attitudes which were as contradictory as the Victorian period itself.

If my father had seen it [Ovid's *Metamorphoses*] in my hands he would have forbidden it to me; which was why I went where I was not likely to be found even if looked for. I was digging away at the myth of Nisus and Scylla, and the purple lock wherein the old king's strength lay, when, for the first time, I was struck by the likeness of this story to that of Samson and Delilah. Hitherto all the Bible stories had been on a raised platform apart, and there was no analogy with them to be found elsewhere. I knew my Ovid pretty well by now; and immediately, on the discovery of this point of resemblance, there flashed across me also the likeness between the story of Myrrha and that of Lot's daughters—of Iphigenia and Isaac for the one part, in the substitution of a doe for the one, of a ram for the other; and of Iphigenia and Jephthah's daughter for the other, where the human element is alone retained. With this my mind went off on the now familiar track of the virgin births, when suddenly—in that strangely rapid and vivid manner in which such things come to me, as if it were really the quick opening of a closed door and the headlong rush into a newly furnished and brilliantly lighted chamber—there shot through my brain these words, which seemed to run along the page in a line of light: "What difference is there between any of these stories and those like to them in the Bible?— . . . between the women made mothers by mysterious influences, and those made mothers by divine favour? between the legends of old times and the stories of Sara, Hannah, Elisabeth—and the Virgin Mary?"

When this last name came, a terrible faintness took hold of me. The perspiration streamed over my face like rain, and I trembled like a frightened horse. My heart, which for a few seconds had beaten like a hammer, now seemed to cease altogether. The light grew dim; the earth was vapoury and unstable; and, overpowered by an awful dread, I fell back among the long grass where I was sitting as if I had been struck down by an unseen hand.[1]

From the city of God, Eliza Lynn turns toward the city of man. Her success in the London publishing world does not mean, however, that she has moved beyond traditional instincts and beliefs. Like Ruskin's contradictory insistences upon woman's traditional place in the home and her reforming duties outside it, Linton's very life is a tangle of paradoxes. She eulogizes the domestic English girl, yet recognizes that she herself is—in the slang of the period—a "revolting daughter." She rejects Christianity, yet takes spiritualism seriously (in fact she claims to have married William James Linton on God's express instructions). As "Mrs. Linton" she proclaims the sanctity of marriage, yet lives apart from her husband. She is one of the first women admitted to the British Museum and writes learned articles and fiction, yet she opposes higher formal education for women. She claims to be the first woman to receive a regular salary as a reporter, yet she insists that the proper sphere of most women is the home.

To appreciate Linton's paradoxical and at times downright perverse habits of mind, we must understand her world, a world dominated by males and male viewpoint. The pressures on young Eliza Lynn would have crushed a less talented and courageous person. She encounters, for example, the brilliant, splenetic editor of the *Morning Chronicle* (and later the *Saturday Review*), John Douglas Cook.

In about half an hour the messenger returned, and ushered me into the awful presence.

For in truth it was an awful presence, in more ways than one. It was not only my hope and present fortune, but of itself, personally, it was formidable. . . .

"So! you are the little girl who has written that queer book [*Amymone*], and want to be one of the press-gang, are you?" he said, half smiling and speaking in a jerky and unprepared manner, both singular and reassuring.

I took him in his humour, and smiled too.

"Yes, I am the woman," I said.

"Woman, you call yourself? I call you a whipper-snapper," he answered, always good-humouredly. "But you seem to have something in you. We'll soon find it out if you have. I say, though, youngster, you never wrote all that rubbish yourself! Some of your brothers helped you. You never scratched all those queer classics and mythology into your own numskull without help. At your age it is impossible."

"It may be impossible," I laughed; "at the same time it is true. I give you my word, no one helped me. No one even saw the manuscript or the proofs," I added eagerly.

On which my new friend and potential master startled me as much as if he had fired off a pistol in my ear, first by his laughter, and then by the volley of oaths which he rolled out—oaths of the strangest compounds and oddest meanings to be heard anywhere—oaths which he himself made at the moment, having a speciality that way unsurpassed, unsurpassable, and inimitable. But as he laughed while he blasphemed, and called me "good girl" in the midst of his wonderful expletives, he evidently did not mean mischief. And I had fortunately enough sense to understand his want of malice, and to accept his manner as of the ordinary course of things.

This pleased him, and after he had exhausted his momentary stock of oaths he clapped me on the back with the force of a friendly sledge-hammer, and said—

"You are a nice kind of little girl, and I think you'll do."

Then he told me to go into the next room to write a leader on a Blue Book which he would send in to me. It was the report of the Parliamentary Commission on the condition of the miners relative to the 'truck' system.

"I give you three hours and a half," he said, taking out his watch. "Not a minute longer, by—. By that time your work must be done, or you'll have no supper to-night! You must take the side of the men; but—d'ye hear?—you are not to assassinate the masters. Leave them a leg to stand on, and don't make Adam Smith turn in his grave by any cursed theories smacking of socialism and the devil knows what. Do you understand, young woman? I have had the passages marked which you are to notice, and so you need not bother that silly cocoanut of yours with any others. Keep to the text; write with strength; and don't talk nonsense. And now be off." (57–59)

She passed the test ("he called me a good girl twenty times" [59]), and she continued to do so for nearly half a century. Although her many novels sell well and have a cultural and biographical interest today, Linton is essentially a journalist who writes reviews and articles on an impressive variety of subjects. With her desire to please dominating males and her willingness to play by the rules of the world, it is not surprising that Eliza Lynn Linton's antifeminist essays defend readily the male-oriented code of social orthodoxy. She spent her daring in the act of survival.

Whatever criticism her particular works received, Linton herself is respected by the London world. Charles Dickens publishes her regularly in *Household Words*; Walter Savage Landor calls her "my dear daughter"; Henry James respects her character if not her characters; and so apparently dissimilar a writer as Algernon Charles Swinburne laments her death in well-intended verse ("Kind, wise, and true as truth's own heart,/A soul . . . Has left us ere we dreamed of death/For life so strong. . . ."[2]). Swinburne's eulogy indicates another important fact about Linton's reputation. It endures beyond the High Victorian period. In the 1890s she is still sought out: by editors, for essays on the New Woman; by interviewers, for periodical pieces and book chapters; and by young writers (particularly women), whom she receives with a warm blend of encouragement and rigour. Mellowness has not dulled the edge of her antifeminism. After forty years of personal success and nearly sixty years of the old Queen's reign, Eliza Lynn Linton can still maintain in 1894 that "we shall go down in the ranks of nations if women ever come to rule us."[3]

I

It was as a controversialist that Eliza Lynn Linton made and sustained her reputation. She tended, like most controversialists, to be extreme, to prefer the polished epigram to the more untidy actualities of a subject. Since "The Girl of the Period" essay goes unquestionably to extremes, that essay shows Linton at her most controversial and influential, but not at her best. "The Modern Revolt" (1870) indicates how complex Linton's vision can be. She defines the woman controversy as both a mad rebellion against natural duties *and* a noble protest against frivolous lives; she recognizes that the desire to enlarge the circle of woman's activities can spring from lofty motives; she admits that "men prefer these living dolls to real women out of fear"; she even maintains that the demand for the franchise is just.[4] At other times Linton can curb her extremism enough to be a deadly critic of the middle class, as her 1868 essay "Modern Mothers" indicates.

> [The Modern Mother] is very sure that nothing improper nor cruel takes place in *her* nursery. Her children do not complain; and she always tells them to come to her when anything is amiss. On which negative evidence she satisfies her soul, and makes sure that all is right because she is too neglectful to see if anything is wrong. She does not remember that her children do not complain because they dare not. Dear and beautiful as all mammas are to the small fry in the nursery, they are always in a certain sense Junos sitting on the top of Mount Olympus, making occasional gracious and benign descents, but practically too far removed for useful interference; while nurse is an ever-present power, capable of sly pinches and secret raids, as well as of more open oppression—a power, therefore, to be propitiated, if only with the grim subservience of a Yezidi too much afraid of the Evil One to oppose him. Wherefore nurse is propitiated, failing the protection of the glorified creature just gone to her grand dinner in a cloud of lace and a blaze of jewels; and the first lesson taught the youthful Christian in short frocks or knickerbockers is not to carry tales down stairs, and by no means to let mamma know what nurse desires should be kept secret.[5]

Here Linton casts an analytical eye upon the bourgeois woman's dream—to become a "lady." Linton defines unflinchingly what the realization of this dream cost the supposed objects of a lady's concern, her children and home. If some Victorians react adversely to "Modern Mothers," others write to *Victoria* praising Linton's perceptions.

> In these days of excitement and pleasure-seeking, when "society" claims more than a reasonable share of [a mother's] time and

attention, the children are left in the charge of hirelings, who are too often neither capable nor willing to do justice to the trust.

The woes of such unfortunate children are graphically described by a writer in the *Saturday Review* of February 29. The article is headed "Modern Mothers," and is well worth a perusal by all philanthropists and social reformers; it depicts in strong colours the evils concerning which I write.[6]

Linton's essay, "The Girl of the Period," sparked furious controversy and imitation. To appreciate the furor, we should begin with the cause.

The Girl of the Period

Time was when the phrase, 'a fair young English girl,' meant the ideal of womanhood; to us, at least, of home birth and breeding. It meant a creature generous, capable, modest; something franker than a Frenchwoman, more to be trusted than an Italian, as brave as an American but more refined, as domestic as a German and more graceful. It meant a girl who could be trusted alone if need be, because of the innate purity and dignity of her nature, but who was neither bold in bearing nor masculine in mind; a girl who, when she married, would be her husband's friend and companion, but never his rival; one who would consider his interests as identical with her own, and not hold him as just so much fair game for spoil; who would make his house his true home and place of rest, not a mere passage-place for vanity and ostentation to pass through; a tender mother, an industrious housekeeper, a judicious mistress.

We prided ourselves as a nation on our women. We thought we had the pick of creation in this fair young English girl of ours, and envied no other men their own. We admired the languid grace and subtle fire of the South; the docility and childlike affectionateness of the East seemed to us sweet and simple and restful; the vivacious sparkle of the trim and sprightly Parisienne was a pleasant little excitement when we met with it in its own domain; but our allegiance never wandered from our brown-haired girls at home, and our hearts were less vagrant than our fancies. This was in the old time, and when English girls were content to be what God and nature had made them. Of late years we have changed the pattern, and have given to the world a race of women as utterly unlike the old insular ideal as if we had created another nation altogether. The Girl of the Period, and the fair young English girl of the past, have nothing in common save ancestry and their mother-tongue; and even of this last the modern version makes almost a new language, through the copious additions it has received from the current slang of the day.

The Girl of the Period is a creature who dyes her hair and paints her face, as the first articles of her personal religion—a creature whose sole idea of life is fun; whose sole aim is unbounded luxury; and whose dress is the chief object of such thought and intellect as she possesses. Her main endeavour is to outvie her neighbours in the extravagance of fashion. No matter if, in the time of crinolines, she sacrifices decency; in the time of trains, cleanliness; in the time of tied-back skirts, modesty; no matter either, if she makes herself a nuisance and an inconvenience to every one she meets;—the Girl of the Period has done away with such moral muffishness as consideration for others, or regard for counsel and rebuke. It was all very well in old-fashioned times, when fathers and mothers had some authority and were treated with respect, to be tutored and made to obey, but she is far too fast and flourishing to be stopped in mid-career by these slow old morals; and as she lives to please herself, she does not care if she displeases every one else.

Nothing is too extraordinary and nothing too exaggerated for her vitiated taste; and things which in themselves would be useful reforms if let alone become monstrosities worse than those which they have displaced so soon as she begins to manipulate and improve. If a sensible fashion lifts the gown out of the mud, she raises hers midway to her knee. If the absurd structure of wire and buckram, once called a bonnet, is modified to something that shall protect the wearer's face without putting out the eyes of her companion, she cuts hers down to four straws and a rosebud, or a tag of lace and a bunch of glass beads. If there is a reaction against an excess of Rowland's Macassar, and hair shiny and sticky with grease is thought less nice than if left clean and healthily crisp, she dries and frizzes and sticks hers out on end like certain savages in Africa, or lets it wander down her back like Madge Wildfire's, and thinks herself all the more beautiful the nearer she approaches in look to a negress or a maniac.

With purity of taste she has lost also that far more precious purity and delicacy of perception which sometimes mean more than appears on the surface. What the *demi-monde* does in its frantic efforts to excite attention, she also does in imitation. If some fashionable *dévergondée en évidence* is reported to have come out with her dress below her shoulder-blades, and a gold strap for all the sleeve thought necessary, the Girl of the Period follows suit next day; and then she wonders that men sometimes mistake her for her prototype, or that mothers of girls not quite so far gone as herself refuse her as a companion for their daughters. She has blunted the fine edges of feeling so much that she cannot understand why she should be condemned for an imitation of form which does not include imitation of fact. She cannot be made to see that modesty of appearance and virtue in deed ought to be inseparable; and that no good girl can afford to appear bad, under pain of receiving the contempt awarded to the bad.

This imitation of the *demi-monde* in dress leads to something in manner and feeling, not quite so pronounced perhaps, but far too like to be honourable to herself or satisfactory to her friends. It leads to slang, bold talk and general fastness; to the love of pleasure and indifference to duty; to the desire of money before either love or happiness; to uselessness at home, dissatisfaction with the monotony of ordinary life, horror of all useful work; in a word, to the worst forms of luxury and selfishness—to the most fatal effects arising from want of high principle and absence of tender feeling.

The Girl of the Period envies the queens of the *demi-monde* far more than she abhors them. She sees them gorgeously attired and sumptuously appointed, and she knows them to be flattered, fêted, and courted with a certain disdainful admiration of which she catches only the admiration while she ignores the disdain. They have all that for which her soul is hungering; and she never stops to reflect at what a price they have bought their gains, and what fearful moral penalties they pay for their sensuous pleasures. She sees only the coarse gilding on the base token, and shuts her eyes to the hideous figure in the midst and the foul legend written round the edge. It is this envy of the pleasures, and indifference to the sins, of these women of the *demi-monde* which is doing such infinite mischief to the modern girl. They brush too closely by each other, if not in actual deeds, yet in aims and feelings; for the luxury which is bought by vice with the one is that thing of all in life most passionately desired by the other, though she is not yet prepared to pay quite the same price. Unfortunately, she has already paid too much—all that once gave her distinctive national character.

No one can say of the modern English girl that she is tender, loving, retiring or domestic. The old fault so often found by keen-sighted Frenchwomen, that she was so fatally *romanesque*, so prone to sacrifice appearances and social advantages for love, will never be set against the Girl of the Period. Love indeed is the last thing she thinks of, and the least of the dangers besetting her. Love in a cottage—that seductive dream which used to vex the heart and disturb the calculations of the prudent mother—is now a myth of past ages. The legal barter of herself for so much money, representing so much dash, so much luxury and pleasure—that is her idea of marriage; the only idea worth entertaining. For all seriousness of thought respecting the duties or the consequences of marriage, she has not a trace. If children come, they find but a stepmother's cold welcome from her; and if her husband thinks that he has married anything that is to belong to him—a *tacens et placens uxor* pledged to make him happy—the sooner he wakes from his hallucination and understands that he has simply married some one who will condescend to spend his money on herself, and who will shelter her indiscretions behind the shield of his name, the less severe will be his disappointment. She has married his house, his carriage, his balance at the banker's, his title; and he himself is just the inevitable condition clogging the wheel of her fortune; at best an adjunct, to be tolerated with more or less patience as may chance. For it is only the old-fashioned sort, not Girls of the Period *pur sang*, who marry for love, or put the husband before the banker. But the Girl of the Period does not marry easily. Men are afraid of her; and with reason. They may amuse themselves with her for an evening, but they do not readily take her for life. Besides, after all her efforts, she is only a poor copy of the real thing; and the real thing is far more amusing than the copy, because it is real. Men can get that whenever they like; and when they go into their mothers' drawing-rooms, with their sisters and their sisters' friends, they want something of quite a different flavour. *Toujours perdrix* is bad providing all the world over; but a continual weak imitation of *toujours perdrix* is worse.

If we must have only one kind of thing, let us have it genuine, and the queens of St. John's Wood in their unblushing honesty rather than their imitators and make-believes in Bayswater and Belgravia. For, at whatever cost of shocked self-love or pained modesty it may be, it cannot be too plainly told to the modern English girl that the net result of her present manner of life is to assimilate her as nearly as possible to a class of women whom we must not call by their proper—or improper—name. And we are willing to believe that she has still some modesty of soul left hidden under all this effrontery of fashion, and that, if she could be made to see herself as she appears to the eyes of men, she would mend her ways before too late.

It is terribly significant of the present state of things when men are free to write as they do of the women of their own nation. Every word of censure flung against them is two-edged, and wounds those who condemn as much as those who are condemned; for surely it need hardly be said that men hold nothing so dear as the honour of their women, and that no one living would willingly lower the repute of his mother or his sisters. It is only when these have placed themselves beyond the pale of masculine respect that such things could be written as are written now. When women become again what they were once they will gather round them the love and homage and chivalrous devotion which were then an Englishwoman's natural inheritance.

The marvel in the present fashion of life among women is, how it holds its ground in spite of the disapprobation of men. It used to be an old-time notion that the sexes were made for each other, and that it was only natural for them to please each other, and to set themselves out for that end. But the Girl of the Period does not please men. She pleases them as little as she elevates them; and how little she does that, the class of women she has taken as her models of itself testifies. All men whose opinion is worth having prefer the simple and genuine girl of the past, with her tender little ways and pretty bashful modesties, to this loud and rampant modernization, with her false red hair and painted skin, talking slang as glibly as a man, and by preference leading the conversation to doubtful subjects. She thinks she is piquante and exciting when she thus makes herself the bad copy of a worse original; and she will not see that though men laugh with her they do not respect her, though they flirt with her they do not marry her; she will not believe that she is not the kind of thing they want, and that she is acting against nature and her own interests when she disregards their advice and offends their taste. We do not understand how she makes out her account, viewing her life from any side; but all we can do is to wait patiently until the national madness has passed, and our women have come back again to the old English ideal, once the most beautiful, the most modest, the most essentially womanly in the world.[7]

II

One way to place "The Girl of the Period" controversy in context is to recognize what Linton did *not* touch primarily upon. The volatile issues of 1868, suffrage, higher education, and unemployment, have little place in the essay. Linton's defense of the True Woman ideal does not take into account, as one contemporary noted, that the ideal is anachronistic in a world where half of all women work and a third never bear children. By establishing as woman's alternatives the melodramatic extremes of angel and demi-mondaine, Linton simply omits (or lumps with the demi-mondaines) that increasing number of respectable women who reject both angel and whore roles and want to extend woman's sphere without forsaking true womanhood. The subject of professionalism appears in

Linton's essays, of course, but the maternal ideal is so rigidly conceived that the essays never give a fair hearing to ideas which are symptomatic of changing times and are considered by some Victorians more important than fashions. Recognition of the special emphasis of "The Girl of the Period" controversy should not, however, obscure one essential fact—the controversy's magnitude. That Linton could ignore so much and still generate such furor indicates how central her worries are to the average Victorian. Concern with women's less than angelic behavior is endemic to the 1860s, as our chapters on Science and on the Sensational and Fleshly Heroines will show (see Volumes II, 2; III, 3, 4). Especially since true womanhood remained—with important modifications—the ideal of most women throughout the rest of the century, Linton clearly speaks to and for many Anglo-American Victorians who sense a cross-cultural decline of values.

"The Girl of the Period" controversy is largely unknown today and has never before been thoroughly researched,[8] but two factors allow us to estimate its magnitude reliably—the number of participants and the variety of offspring. "Perhaps the most sensational middle article that the *Saturday Review* ever published," Linton's essay then appears as a pamphlet which sells forty thousand copies for one printer alone.[9] Victorians correctly see it as an "epoch making essay."[10] For the amused middle and upper classes, the G.O.P. (as it came to be known) "made a famous topic of conversation at dinner-tables."[11] These classes, however, worry righteously about the article's impact upon the lower orders.

> The writer of the article no doubt meant it for a mere piece of rhetorical exaggeration, assuming that those who were likely to read it would be able to make the necessary qualifications for themselves; but we fear that it has been the cause of much mischief elsewhere than in India, especially since its circulation in a cheap form has made it accessible to a class of readers who are without the special knowledge which would enable them to distinguish between the basis of fact and the superstructure of imaginative satire. Such readers may be roughly divided into *imitators* and *abhorrers*, the former being much the larger class, if we take in all who secretly and inwardly worship an idol which they conceive to be fashionable life, while the latter and noisier class are mostly under the same magnetic influence (though for the moment it may show itself in repulsion rather than attraction), and would be ready, with a little encouragement, to pass over to the other side. What can be worse

for the one than to have a vicious and coarse vulgarity held out as the pattern they should aim at; or, for the other, than to have fresh fuel for the hatred which they feel or affect to feel towards all that is more favoured by fortune?[12]

The reference to India indicates that the G.O.P. reaches readers and provokes controversy far beyond England. In September of 1868, *Victoria* prints the following notice:

> The Girl of the Period.—An Irish lady, writing from the centre of India, says: "Did you see that article in the *Saturday Review* some time ago, called 'The Girl of the Period?' It was spiteful and untrue; but Captain ____ tells me that it has done an immense deal of harm out here. It has been translated into Hindostani, and the people are all saying, 'Why should they educate their women if that's the result of education on English women?'"[13]

On the other side of the world, America is reprinting the *Saturday Review* articles and is following the social furor through the London correspondents of the *New York Times* (particularly "Monadnock"). On August 27, 1868, for example, Americans learn that the "articles upon women have excited a good deal of indignation" and that "The *Saturday's* remarks about women are acknowledged to be true of some." A full year later the announcement of a furious counterattack by M.E. Braddon indicates how newsworthy the G.O.P. remained.[14]

Nearly as numerous as Linton's readers are her offspring. The expression "The Girl of the Period" gave rise to "The Paradox of the Period," "the ordinary muttonchop of the period," "The Cigar of the Period," "The Poetry of the Period," "The Reviewer of the Period," "The Shakespeare of the Period," "A Wife of the Period," "A School-Girl of the Period," "The Children of the Period," "The Roman Girl of the Period," "The Girl of the Future," "The Dangerous Woman of the Period," "The Past and Future Girl of the Period," "Puffs of the Period." After the "Girl of the Period" essay came *The Girl of the Period Miscellany, The Girl of the Period Almanac, The Girl of the Period Songster*, plus Alfred Austin's acerbic *The Poetry of the Period*.[15] Nor are all the offspring literary. G.O.P. parasols and clothing become the rage. A subfuror over The Waist of the Period prompts *Tomahawk* to quip:

> A correspondence is at this moment raging on the subject of the "Waist of the Period!" *Cui bono?* Surely every day proves that the real *waste* of the period, as far as woman is concerned, is—words![16]

Besides the labored Joke of the Period, one-liners are sparked:

> Since the "Girl of the Period," as depicted by the writer in the *Saturday Pooh-pooh* is entirely an imaginary creation on the part of that writer, it follows, as a matter of course, that he himself must be a miss-creant!
>
> WHERE A FULL STOP IS WANTED.—To the Girl of the Period.[17]

Also amusing is the Muse.

> *AN APROPOS SOLILOQUY.*
> *By a Girl of the Period.*
>
> To dye, or not to dye, that is the question:—
> "Whether 'tis nobler in the mind, to suffer"
> Th' outrageous colour of Dame Nature born,
> The very "head and front of my offending"
> Against the fist of chameleon Fashion,
> Or summon Art to aid me? Shall I end
> This heart-ache by the "hazard of a dye"
> That Fashion dooms my hair to?—Dye:—a wash:—
> No more:—Poison, perhaps? ay, that's the rub
> To bring paralysis. . . .[18]

As this example indicates, satire frequently finds dramatic form. Not only do Mr. Punch and his peers feature comic dialogues frequently, but one of the period's most successful dramatists, F.C. Burnand, stages a burlesque, *The Girls of the Period*, during the Christmas holidays of 1868–69.

> Scene II.—The Island of Nowarpartickilar, on the Thames. ["On my Island there's a club of Girls of the Period—and on the boundaries is placed a notice 'All *men* landing here will be prosecuted as trespassers. By order of Calypso, Queen of the Girls of the Period.'"] Music opening to A. Sullivan's "Contra-bandista."—(Boosey and Sons.)
>
> *The* GIRLS OF THE PERIOD, *with preparations for pic-nic, discovered listening.*
> *Enter* MISS CALYPSO—*they salute her.*
>
>
> CALY. Girls of the Period! Here we're met in session,
>   To give our opinions free expression.

ALL. We are, we are!
CALY.   Who would be free, you know,
  The poet says, themselves must strike the blow.
ALL. Brava! brava!
CALY.   Consider, what's our mission—
  To elevate the feminine condition—
  To show that man shall not our master be.
ALL. Hear. hear.
CALY.   To show that we're as good as he—
ALL. And better.
CALY. Aye, and better.   'Tis all fudge,
  To think a girl a mere domestic drudge;
  Born to be schooled, and ruled, and fooled—
ALL.   No, no.
CALY. That we are not so, we are here to show.
  Our right to row, race, ride, bowl, shoot, and smoke,
  We will establish here beyond a joke.
  And, more than that, the notion up has grown
  That only man can go about *alone*.
ALL. Yah!

[Telemachus Brown, chafing against the boredom of marriage, and his bachelor friend Coelebs Robinson, a Young Man of the Period, have gone out seeking adventure and have landed on Nowarpartickilar. Telemachus' wife, his mother-in-law, and his former tutor, Dr. Mentor, follow and are helped by Calypso to win Telemachus back.]

Ballet of The Girls of the Period.

COEL. (*to* TELEMACHUS, L.C.) Well, isn't this delicious? You don't regret having come out for a holiday?
TEL. Yes, I do. If this is the Girl of the Period, give me the Wife of the Period, I mean my own.
MRS. T. (L.C.) Your own? Nonsense, you've got none. Besides, you're to be won without wooing.
CALY. Yes, we've put you two down as prizes. All the girls have entered. . . .
TEL. Oh! I'm to be run for, am I?
CALY. Yes, in our Derby of the Period.
COEL. Ah! but where are the horses?
DR. M. (R.) Dear me, young man, you're very much behind your age. The Derby of the Period is run on velocipedes.
TEL. But you don't mean that the girls——
DR. M. Yes, sir; there is more in heaven and earth, Horatio, than is dreamt of in your velocipede.
Music—enter the GIRLS *on velocipedes.* . . .

"THE GIRL OF THE PERIOD!"
OR,
PAINTED BY A PRURIENT PRUDE

5. The Girl of the Period; or, Painted by a Prurient Prude
The Tomahawk, 1868

The Velocipede Race is run and the winner [Mrs. T.] *is cheered.* [She chooses T., Caly, takes Coel.]

MRS. T. Well, do you prefer me as a Girl of the Period, or——

TEL. No, as the military word of command is, "as you were."

CALY. (coming down c.) No, Mr. Coelebs, I'm very much flattered by the offer, but at present I can't decide—my reign on the Island of Nowarpartickilar is not yet at an end, but you may look in here again, and if you are still of the same mind, then I may perhaps abdicate, and cease to be the QUEEN OF THE GIRLS OF THE PERIOD[19]

Finally, plain (sometimes positively sharp) English prose is addressed to a variety of the G.O.P.'s social offshoots—by *Punch* and *Fun*.

"LOOK AT THE CLOCK"
(Caution to Modistes, Milliners, et id genus omne.)

A Leicester Square Dressmaker was summoned and fined last week, under the Act in that case made and provided for working a dozen of her young ladies over-hours. She pleaded a large order from Drury Lane for "Girls of the Period." Mr. Tyrwhite very properly decided that employers must not work "Girls of the Period," over the period—fixed by the statute; and fined Madame 40s. and costs, with the remark that "he had no notion of work-people being made slaves of." Mr. Punch has a notion that this class of workpeople are made slaves of, very often, and rejoices accordingly whenever the Emancipation Act is brought to bear on the slave-driver.

THE SATURDAY SHREW.

The *Saturday Review* the other day acknowledged the existence of "good girls of the real old English type." The sixpenny show of journalism has railed at women so long that perhaps when it grants thus much we ought not to look the gift in the mouth: Still we should like to know the exact meaning of "the old English type." Perhaps the middle-aged dame who has thus scolded so because girls will be pretty, means "old-faced type." If we are to go back to the very old English, all we can say is that, unless history tells fibs, the girls of that period used to paint—a very bright blue. But then, to be sure, in the matter of dress there was not much to take hold of.[20]

The G.O.P. is a major cultural moment because its protean offspring and international readership involve more than simply witty (and not so witty) foolishness. Linton's articles appear at the moment when a long-heated cauldron is ready to boil over. The *Saturday Review* had fed the flame for more than a decade, creating enemies by castigating whatever splenetic John Douglas Cook thought false or pretentious. When it begins its attack upon women by focusing on her clothes ("Costume and Its Morals"), the *Saturday Review* fuels an already heated controversy—with *Punch* ridiculing the crinoline, doctors warning against tight-lacing and stiff stays, and everyone bemoaning the chignon.[21] Although reactions run heavily against Linton's view of English Womanhood, the very intensity of the counterattacks indicates how threatened many Victorians feel. As several of the most candid reviewers say (with more accuracy than originality), "There is no smoke without fire."[22]

A whole anthology could be devoted simply to the responses to Linton's articles. Most commentators (excepting those outraged about outraged womanhood) were fairly sanguine, maintaining that the *Saturday Review* had taken traits from various female types and combined them into an unrepresentative monstress, that the decade was if anything more genteel than pre-Victorian times, and that the era, as transitional, would inevitably produce a few anomalies but would just as inevitably manage to combine increased freedom with traditional womanly virtues. The most persistent commentators upon the G.O.P. are the satirical magazines. *Punch, Judy, Fun,* and *Tomahawk* exercise their jester's prerogative of having things both ways. They attack the foibles of women and yet defend womankind against the *Saturday Review*.[23] The satirical magazines are also first to put the shoe on the other foot. As early as May 9, 1868, *Fun* contrasts majestic womanhood with that ridiculous spindly-legged and monocled creature, the Young Man of the Period. Excellent cartoons follow in *Judy* and *Tomahawk,* plus a long letter from Mrs. Punch, and a *Judy* poem that begins

THE YOUNG MAN OF THE PRESENT DAY
By One of the Opposite Sex

Once, with a bright, brief petticoat, and manner unmethodical,
I was "the girl of the period"—and of the periodical;
But now they've given me up for bad, and 't seems we at war to be
With "the young man of the present day," who isn't what he ought
to be. [24]

The charges against Linton are basically three. Most serious is a failure of sympathy. Victorians worry increasingly that social changes—particularly rising standards of luxury—are making young men less inclined to marry and are thus making young women more desperate and forward. J.B. Mayors, for example, discusses "the effects of the increasing uncertainty of marriage, and the disadvantageous position of single women, with reference particularly to those who accept the circumstances in which they find themselves, and enter with keener competition into the struggle as the prize becomes more difficult of attainment." Mayors concludes humanely: "The change in the manners of girls may be partly accounted for by the keener competition for matrimony and the immensely-widened compass of society."[25] Linton's failure to appreciate that marriage has become a positively Darwinian struggle for women is a charge made not only by the popular "Two Girls of the Period," but also by the best early review of the G.O.P. Henry James, reviewing *Modern Women and What Is Said of Them*, recognizes compassionately that "it is a very dismal truth that the only hope of most women, at the present moment, for a life worth the living, lies in marriage, and marriage with rich men or men likely to become so, and that in their unhappy weakness they often betray an ungraceful anxiety on this point."[26]

The two other widespread charges against Linton also appear in James's review. That Linton exaggerated woman's foibles, virtually everyone agrees. Most writers also agree with M.E. Braddon's answer to the question "who taught the girls of England this hateful slang? who showed them . . . these odious women? Who, indeed, but the men, who now recoil from the work of their own hands."[27] These two charges are made effectively by Henry James because he possesses the careful moderate vision which "The Girl of the Period" essay lacks. "The attempts to draw an idle smile at the expense of poor girls apprehensive of spinsterhood is, therefore, not a very creditable one" (333). James places the blame elsewhere. Men "give the *ton*—they pitch the key."

> The *Saturday Review* has had the credit of having shown us how good the social article can be; but it seems also to have been disposed to show us how bad. Singly, as they came out, these pieces may have appeared to possess a certain brilliancy and vigor, and, at a stretch, one can imagine them to have furnished a group of idle people, of unformed taste, a theme for ten minutes' talk.

But it is as incredible that, as we are told, they should have produced a sensation then as it is that they should produce a revolution now. The authorship of the papers we have no means of knowing. We gather from intrinsic evidence that they are the product of several hands—in one of which, at least, we certainly detect the feminine *griffe*. But if they differ somewhat in tone, they differ imperceptibly in merit. They are all equally trivial, commonplace, and vulgar. The vulgarity of thought, indeed, which they display, the absence of reflection, observation, and feeling, of substance, of style, and of grace, and the manner in which the thinnest and crudest literary flippancy and colloquial slanginess are thrust forward in the place of these sacred essentials, is, when one considers their pretensions, the character of their subject, and the superior auspices under which they were ushered into the world, an almost inconceivable spectacle. . . .

The American reader will be struck by the remoteness and strangeness of the writer's tone and allusions. He will see that the society which makes these papers even hypothetically—hyperbolically—possible is quite another society from that of New York and Boston. American life, whatever may be said, is still a far simpler process than the domestic system of England. We never read a good English novel (and much more a bad one), we never read either Mr. Trollope or Mr. Trollope's inferiors, without drawing a long breath of relief at the thought of all that we are spared, and without thanking fortune that we are not part and parcel of that dark, dense British social fabric. An American is born into a so much simpler world; he inherits so many less obligations, conventions, and responsibilities. And so with the American girl. You have only to reflect how her existence, in comparison with that of her British sister, is simplified at a stroke by the suppression in this country of that distinguished being the "eldest son," of that romantic class the "younger sons." Another cause of greater complexity in life for Englishmen and English girls alike is their immediate proximity to that many-colored Continent, of which we, in comparison, have the means to learn so little. And this brings us back to the "Girl of the Period." This young lady, we are assured, is, in England, an exact reproduction, in appearance and manners, of a Parisian *cocotte*—or whatever the latest term may be. If this is not true, it is at least slightly plausible. Irregular society, in France, has become so extensive and aggressive that he who runs—and she who walks—may easily read its minutest features. An English girl who makes with her parents a regular autumnal trip to the Continent encounters face to face, in all the great cities, at all the chief watering-places, the celebrities—and indeed the obscurities—of the *demi-monde*. The theory of the Saturday Reviewer is that familiarity breeds not contempt, but emulation. Whatever may be the worth of his theory, his description of the young lady thus demoralized is decidedly vigorous. She is a painted, powdered, "enamelled" creature, stained with belladonna and antimony, crowned with a shock of false hair, wearing her walking-dress indecently high and her evening dress abominably low. She has no manners and no feelings, and only brains enough to ensnare a rich husband. She frankly sells her self; she marries for money, without a semblance of sentiment or romance. The relation of the Girl of the Period to marriage forms, under one aspect or another, the subject of the greater number of the ensuing articles. We find it reiterated, of course, with emphasis, that to marry, and to marry well, is the one great object of young girls' energies and desires. According as a girl marries or not, life is a prize or a blank. Innumerable arts, therefore, are practised both by the young ladies and their mothers, cunning machinations are devised, in the interest of this sacred need. It is all a very old story, and English novels have long since made us acquainted with it: how a match-making matron fixes her cold, magnetic eye upon the unsuspecting possessor of a comfortable income—how, with her daughter's aid and the insidious help of picnics and croquet and musical parties, she weaves about him the undisseverable web of a presumptive engagement, and finally leads him, muddled, confused, and bullied, to the altar. The various tricks of the marriage-market are enumerated with a bold, unpitying crudity. It is a very dismal truth that the only hope of most women, at the present moment, for a life worth the living, lies in marriage, and marriage with rich men or men likely to become so, and that in their unhappy weakness they often betray an ungraceful anxiety on this point. But to our minds there is nothing comical in the situation, and as a field for satirical novelists it has ceased to be actively worked. The attempt to draw an idle smile at the expense of poor girls apprehensive of spinsterhood is, therefore, not a very creditable one. On all other points women receive here equally hard measure. Some of the accusations touch, doubtless, upon real foibles and follies, but others seem to us thoroughly beside the mark. . . .

What do you see when on a clear autumn day you measure the length of the Fifth Avenue, or ascend the sunny slope of Beacon Street? Do you encounter a train of youthful Jezebels with plastered faces and lascivious eyes and a general *dévergondage* of mien? You meet a large number of very pretty and, on the whole, very fresh-looking girls, dressed in various degrees of the prevailing fashion. It is obvious that their persons betray a very lively desire to be well dressed, and that the idea "well dressed" has, to their minds, a peculiar significance. It has a sacred and absolute meaning. Their bonnets must be very small, their panniers very large, their heels very high, and all their appointments as elegant as possible. A young girl of fashion dressed to suit her own taste is undeniably a very artificial and composite creature, and doubtless not an especially edifying spectacle. She has largely compromised her natural freedom of movement. The most that you can say of her is that she is charming, with a *quasi*-corrupt arbitrary charm. She has, moreover, great composure and impenetrability of aspect. She practises a sort of half-cynical indifference to the beholder (we speak of the extreme cases). Accustomed to walk alone in the streets of a great city, and to be looked at by all sorts of people, she has acquired an unshrinking directness of gaze. She is the least bit *hard*. If she is more than this—if she is painted and touzled and wantonly *chiffonnée*—she is simply an exception, and the sisterhood of "modern women" are in no way responsible for her. She would have been the same in the good old times of our great-grand-mothers. The faults and follies that can be really fastened upon the younger women of the present day are, in our opinion, all caused and explained by the growing love of luxury and elegance. The standard in these matters is so much higher than it was thirty and forty years ago that a young girl—even when she has money—needs a great deal more time to maintain herself at the proper level. She has frequently no time left for anything else—for study, for reflection, or sentiment. She is absorbed in the care of her person. A young girl given up to dress is certainly a very flimsy and empty creature, and there is something truly ignoble in the incessant effort to gratify and stimulate the idle taste of a host of possible "admirers." But between this sort of thing and the sort of thing described by the Saturday Reviewers there is a very wide gulf—a gulf made by that strong conservative element in the feminine nature of which the writer in question seems to have so little notion. Women turn themselves into painted courtesans for two reasons—as a means of gaining a subsistence which is impracticable in any other way or because they have a natural taste for the business. The first motive is common, and the second is rare; so rare that where the first does not exist, the *rapprochement* of the Saturday Reviewer is a wanton exaggeration in the interest of sensationalism. The whole indictment represented by this volume seems to us perfectly irrational. It is impossible to discuss and condemn the follies of "modern women" apart from those of modern men. They are all part and parcel of the follies of modern civilization, which is working itself out through innumerable blunders. It seems to us supremely absurd to stand up in the high places and endeavor, with a long lash and a good deal of bad language, to drive women back into the ancient fold. Their extravagance is a part of their increased freedom, and their increased freedom a part of the growth of society. The lamentable results—the extremely uncomfortable "wreck" society would be sure to incur from an attempt to fasten again upon womankind the tether which was sufficient unto the aspirations of Miss Hannah More and Miss Edgeworth, the authors of these papers would be the first to denounce. We are all of us extravagant, superficial, and luxurious together. It is a "sign of the times." Women share in the fault not as women, but as simple human beings. As women, they strike us as still remarkably patient, submissive, sympathetic—remarkably well-disposed to model themselves on the judgment and wishes of men. They reflect with great clearness the state of the heart and imagination of men. When they present an ugly picture, therefore, we think it the part of wisdom for men to cast a glance at their own internal economy. If there is any truth in the volume before us, they have a vast deal to answer for. They give the *ton*—they pitch the key. (332–34)

Finally, an 1868 excerpt from *Victoria* indicates how beset the woman of advanced ideas finds herself. She has to battle not only enemies but friends. Chauvinism is dangerous, but paternalism is probably worse. Responding to a condescension which never acknowledges that the Woman Question involves anything more than a graceful repetition of platitudes, *Victoria* attacks defenders of woman—in the name of woman. And manifests how complicated the debate is.

. . . there has appeared in the *St. Paul's Magazine* for June a paper entitled the "Women of the Day," in which the Saturday defamers are pretty well castigated. But the writer fails to search deeply into causes, or we should rather say openly declares his disinclination to do more than meet and confute the reviewers on the surface of the question. Excellent in intention, we must regret the extreme shallowness of this reply, and enter our protest against the contented after-dinner style of the well-to-do conventional Briton, so manifest throughout. No better proof can be afforded of the light in which women are regarded by men of a large class in this country, than in the kindly-patronising, superior, protecting manner of some passages which follow:—
"The *Saturday Review*, as far as my own observation goes, is, I should say, a paper which numbers amongst its readers an unusually large proportion of the female sex. Its politics—if I may venture to say so—are of an eminently female order; its cleverness just of the kind which women think very clever; and its satire is of a calibre which women can understand and appreciate. A very slight knowledge of the female nature was sufficient to justify the conviction that tirades against women would find an attentive if not sympathetic feminine audience. . . . But like children, they would sooner be teased than not noticed at all. Indeed the very fact of

attack is a covert compliment to their paramount influence and importance."

It is sincerely to be hoped, before many generations have passed away, such time-worn sickening platitudes regarding women may have bleated and brayed themselves into eternal silence. Nursery rhymes of "women and walnut trees," with other traditional, nonsensical, and fabulous stories of infancy, have had too long a day, and could well have been put aside by the comfortable, conventional *litterateur* of *St. Paul's*. Drivelling stuff like this could never have been talked had women enjoyed their just rights and legal privileges, instead of being sunk into a servile and despicable position by the thoughtlessness, ignorance, and selfishness of men.

"The reviewer thinks that English ladies are no better than they ought to be. I think they are quite as good as can be expected." We have nothing to say against this cool decision and commendation, but the writer is surely bound after such declaration to explain it in a reasonable manner. Cant simpering of the comfortable *paterfamilias* comes out strongly and offensively here.

"Women, all the world over, are by no means very angry with those who attack them—they understand the flattery which lies hid beneath the sneer; and they know that the irritation of their assailants, like the anger of a pet spaniel, can always be subdued by alternate slaps and caresses."

There is an obvious fallacy in the following sentences, for the highest and best education, rendering the mind broader and more philosophic, would teach women to find the greatest pleasure and content in the first and most essential duties of life. At present their flimsy meretricious mental training renders them incapable of correctly estimating the value and importance of rightly fulfilling such duties.

"Our women know more, read more, think more than they did in the good old days, and we cannot reasonably expect that they should be contented with the same narrow round of pleasures and duties. . . . In virtue of that principle we have to a great extent exempted women from household and menial cares: and by so doing we have secured a degree of culture and refinement not compatible, I think, with any very active interference in domestic matters. . . . I hold that we are unreasonable in expecting that English ladies should unite the inconsistent merits of the intellectual companion and the business housewife."

And finally our good old English gentleman shirks the main question, fearing possibly a derangement of the digestive organs might be the result of deep inquiry.

"That Englishwomen have faults, no candid judge would pretend to deny. [This is very wise and to the point.] How far these faults are due to defective education, to unequal social conditions, or to natural qualities, is a point on which I am not sure that I have any positive opinion, and on which I am certainly not going to express any opinion."

But we will not weary our readers with further extracts from a writer who lacks originality of thought as much as gracefulness of expression.[28]

The G.O.P. controversy indicates how close to the surface Victorian anxiety was, and how important surfaces were as indices of deepseated forces. To understand these forces, however, Victorians had to go beyond fashion and manners and confront the impact upon women of such enormous social realities as law, science, work, and religion.

Notes

For long quotations, references are given first to pages from which quotation has been made; inclusive page numbers for the entire article are given in square brackets.

Chapter 1

[1]"To Maria Lewis," September 17, 1840, *The George Eliot Letters,* ed. Gordon S. Haight, I (New Haven: Yale Univ. Press, 1954), 66.

[2]Publisher's Notice, *Woman's Mission* (Boston, 1840). Except for the publisher's notice and a review by T.M. Rearden in the 1841 *Congregational Magazine* describing Lewis as "a lady known in episcopalian circles," no biographical information has been located. The *Wellesley Index* names Lewis as the author of an article on governesses; see *Fraser's*, 37 (1848), 411–14. References to *Woman's Mission*, which have been taken from the 1840 Boston edition, will be incorporated into the text.

[3]Between 1834 and 1847, five editions of *De l'education des mères de famille* were issued in France; for a favorable response in England, see *Westminster Review*, 22 (1835), 504–10. In 1842 Edwin Lee produced an English translation, *The Education of Mothers of Families*, which was reprinted in a cheaper edition; an American edition of Lee's translation appeared in 1843. *Woman's Mission* was even more popular. By 1842, J.W. Parker published the tenth English edition, and Wiley issued the fourth American edition. By 1854 the book reached its seventeenth English edition and its fifth American.

[4]"To Maria Lewis," October 27, 1840, *Letters*, I, 72. Bonnie Zimmerman discusses Eliot's reading of the French and English texts in "'The Mother's

History' in George Eliot's Life, Literature, and Political Ideology," in *The Lost Tradition: Mothers and Daughters in Literature*, ed. Cathy Davidson and E.M. Broner (New York: Ungar, 1980).

⁵For further information on the intellectual, social, and political issues affecting American women during the 1830s, see Nancy F. Cott, *The Bonds of Womanhood: "Woman's Sphere" in New England, 1780–1835* (New Haven: Yale Univ. Press, 1977); Carl N. Degler, *At Odds: Women and the Family in America from the Revolution to the Present* (New York: Oxford Univ. Press, 1980); Keith E. Melder, *The Beginnings of Sisterhood: The American Woman's Rights Movement, 1800–1850* (New York: Schocken, 1977) and "Ladies Bountiful: Organized Women's Benevolence in Early 19th Century America," *New York History*, 48 (1967), 231–54. For the intellectual and political climate in England, see John Killham, *Tennyson and "The Princess": Reflections of an Age* (London: Athlone Press, 1968), esp. Chs. 5 and 6; and Dorothy Thompson, "Women and Nineteenth Century Radical Politics," in *The Rights and Wrongs of Women*, ed. Juliet Mitchell and Ann Oakley (Harmondsworth, Middlesex: Penguin, 1976).

⁶*Liberator*, July 13, 1833, p. 111. Important studies of women abolitionists include Blanche Glassman Hersh, *The Slavery of Sex: Feminist-Abolitionists in America* (Urbana: Univ. of Illinois Press, 1978); Aileen Kraditor, *Means and Ends in American Abolitionism* (New York: Pantheon, 1969); and Alma Lutz, *Crusade for Freedom: Women of the Antislavery Movement* (Boston: Beacon Press, 1968). In *The Remembered Gate: Origins of American Feminism* (New York: Oxford Univ. Press, 1978), Barbara Berg argues that feminism is not rooted in the abolitionist movement, but rather in female voluntary associations that flourished in America after 1800.

⁷Quoted in Melder, *The Beginnings of Sisterhood*, p. 75.

⁸Consult Gerda Lerner, *The Grimké Sisters from South Carolina: Rebels Against Slavery* (Boston: Houghton Mifflin, 1967). Excerpts from *Letters on the Equality of the Sexes* are analyzed in Vol. II, Ch. 2.

⁹[Margaret Mylne], "Woman, and Her Social Position," *Westminster Review*, 35 (1841), 24.

¹⁰[Jeremy Bentham and T.P. Thompson], "The Greatest Happiness Principle," *Westminster Review*, 11 (1829), 266; [William Fox], "A Political and Social Anomaly," *Monthly Repository*, 6 (1832), 637–42; "An Outline of the Grievances of Women," *Metropolitan Magazine*, 22 (1838), 16–22. The women's petition is reprinted in Patricia Hollis' *Women in Public, 1850–1900* (London: Allen and Unwin, 1979), pp. 288–89.

¹¹[Harriet Martineau], "The Martyr Age of the United States," *Westminster Review*, 32 (1838), 1–59. Norton's legal reforms are discussed in Vol. II, Ch. 1.

¹²E.P. Thompson discusses "time-discipline" and "task-orientation" in "Time, Work-Discipline, and Industrial Capitalism," *Past and Present*, 38 (1967), 56–98; on pp. 51–62 of *The Bonds of Womanhood*, Cott uses these concepts to analyze woman's sphere. For nineteenth-century theories of child development, see Anne L. Kuhn, *The Mother's Role in Childhood Education: New England Concepts, 1830–1860* (New Haven: Yale Univ. Press, 1947), esp. Part 2.

¹³*Godey's Lady's Book*, January 20, 1840, p. 95; rev. of *Woman's Mission*, *Athenaeum*, July 6, 1839, p. 503; [T.H. Lister], "Rights and Condition of Women," *Edinburgh Review*, 73 (1841), 190; [Mylne], p. 29.

¹⁴Marion Reid (Mrs. Hugo Reid), *A Plea for Women*, ed. Caroline May Kirkland (New York, 1845), p. 14. Later references to this American edition will be incorporated into the text.

¹⁵[Anna Jameson], "Condition of the Women and the Female Children," *Athenaeum*, March 18, 1843, p. 257; this essay is analyzed in Vol. II, Ch. 3.

¹⁶Rev. of *Woman's Mission, Westminster Review*, 34 (1840), 254–57. For the most rhapsodic response to Lewis' text, see [— Adams], *Westminster Review*, 52 (1850), 352–78. Charlotte Brontë's comment on the review is contained in her letter "To Elizabeth Gaskell," August 27, 1850, *The Brontës: Their Lives, Friendships and Correspondence*, ed. T.J. Wise and J.A. Symington (Oxford: Shakespeare Head, 1931–38), III, 149–50.

¹⁷A Plea for Woman was originally published in 1843 by William Tait in Edinburgh; it was reviewed favorably in *Tait's Edinburgh Magazine*, NS 11 (1844), 423–28; and in the *Athenaeum*, March 2, 1844, pp. 189–90, and March 9, 1844, pp. 215–17. *A Plea* seems to have sold better in America than in Britain; five American editions were published between 1847 and 1852. Such later feminists as Caroline Dall and Helen Blackburn recognized the importance of Reid's ideas.

¹⁸History of Woman Suffrage, ed. Elizabeth Cady Stanton, Susan B. Anthony, and Matilda Joslyn Gage, I (New York, 1881), 59. George Harvey is identified by C. Duncan Rice in *The Scots Abolitionists, 1833–1861* (Baton Rouge: Louisiana State Univ. Press, 1981), p. 89. On the interaction of British and American women at this convention, see Betty Fladeland, *Men and Brothers: Anglo-American Anti-Slavery Cooperation* (Urbana: Univ. of Illinois Press, 1972), pp. 178–79, 258–69; Frederick B. Tolles, ed., *Slavery and the "Woman Question": Lucretia Mott's Diary of Her Visit to Great Britain to Attend the World's Anti-Slavery Convention of 1840* (Haverford, Pa.: Friends Historical Association, 1952); and Elizabeth Cady Stanton, *Eighty Years and More* (London, 1898), pp. 80–83.

¹⁹Legal similarities between women and blacks are discussed in Vol. II, Ch. 1; "scientific" arguments regarding their similarities, in Vol. II, Ch. 2.

²⁰The attempt to improve women's lives by accepting and then extending the concept of woman's mission is sometimes called Domestic Feminism. During the past decade, numerous studies have analyzed its practical consequences, particularly in America. In *Catharine Beecher: A Study in American Domesticity* (New Haven: Yale Univ. Press, 1973), Kathryn Kish Sklar explains how the American educator used the doctrine of the spheres to improve women's education *and* to confine them to certain vocations; see esp. Chs. 9–12. Carroll Smith-Rosenberg shows how a basically conservative group applied the ideology during their 1830s crusade against sexual abuse in "Beauty, the Beast, and the Militant Woman," *American Quarterly*, 23 (1971), 562–84. In *The Clubwoman as Feminist: True Womanhood Redefined, 1868–1914* (New York: Holmes and Meier, 1980), Karen Blair describes the ways in which literary clubwomen used their special qualities as ladies to enter the public domain. Barbara Leslie Epstein takes a more critical stance toward the separate spheres in *The Politics of Domesticity: Women, Evangelism, and Temperance in Nineteenth-Century America* (Middletown, Conn.: Wesleyan Univ. Press, 1981), as does Joan N. Burstyn in *Victorian Education and the Ideal of Womanhood* (London: Croom Helm, 1980).

²¹"A Woman's Thoughts About Women," *Saturday Review*, 5 (1858), 377.

Chapter 2

¹William Thompson, *Appeal of One Half the Human Race, Women, against the Pretensions of the Other Half, Men, to Restrain Them in Political and thence Civil and Domestic Slavery; in Reply to Mr. Mill's Celebrated "Article on Government"* (London,

1825; rpt. New York: Burt Franklin, 1970, and Source Book Press, 1970).

²R.K.P. Pankhurst, *William Thompson* (London: Watts, 1954), p. 6. Except for Pankhurst's excellent book, there has been virtually no work done on Thompson's feminism. See Marian Ramelson, *The Petticoat Rebellion* (London: Lawrence and Wishart, 1967), pp. 58–62; Constance Rover, *Love, Morals and the Feminists* (London: Routledge & Kegan Paul, 1970), pp. 26–28; Sheila Rowbotham, *Hidden from History* (New York: Pantheon, 1974), pp. 39–41.

³Pankhurst, p. 12.

⁴James Mill's "Article on Government" appeared first in 1820, in Volume IV of the *Supplement* to the fifth edition of the *Encyclopedia Britannica*. After publication in pamphlet form in 1821, it was reprinted later in the 1820s in two collections of Mill's essays, plus in the 1825 pamphlet and the collected *Supplement* of 1824. The most available source of the essay today contains also the famous reply by Macaulay: *Utilitarian Logic and Politics*, ed. Jack Lively and John Rees (Oxford: Clarendon, 1978). Mill's offending passage on women appears on p. 79 of this edition.

⁵Pankhurst, p. 80.

⁶John Stuart Mill, *On Liberty* (London, 1859).

⁷Pankhurst, p. 75. For a much more negative view of Wheeler, see Michael Sadleir's *Bulwer: A Panorama: Edward & Rosina, 1803–1836* (London: Constable, 1931), pp. 67–72, 128, and Louisa Davey's *Life of Rosina, Lady Lytton* (London, 1887), pp. 5–7.

⁸John Stuart Mill, *Autobiography* (London, 1873; reprinted, New York: Bobbs-Merrill, 1957), p. 80.

⁹Henry James, *The Portrait of a Lady* (London, 1881), Ch. 42.

Chapter 3

¹Henry James, *William Wetmore Story and His Friends* (Boston: Houghton Mifflin, 1903), I, 131.

²Ibid., I, 127.

³Ralph Waldo Emerson, W.H. Channing, and James Freeman Clarke, eds., *Memoirs of Margaret Fuller Ossoli* (London, 1852), 3 vols. Recent studies against which the *Memoirs* should be read include Paula Blanchard, *Margaret Fuller* (New York: Delacorte/Seymour Lawrence, 1978); Bell Gale Chevigny, *The Woman and the Myth: Margaret Fuller's Life and Writings* (Old Westbury, N.Y.: Feminist Press, 1976); Margaret Vanderhaar Allen, *The Achievement of Margaret Fuller* (University Park: Pennsylvania State Univ. Press, 1979); and the chapters on Fuller in Susan Phinney Conrad, *Perish the Thought: Intellectual Women in Romantic America, 1830–1860* (New York: Oxford Univ. Press, 1976); Ann Douglas, *The Feminization of American Culture* (New York: Knopf, 1977); and Barbara Welter, *Dimity Convictions: The American Woman in the Nineteenth Century* (Athens: Ohio Univ. Press, 1976).

⁴The *Memoirs* received at least forty reviews or notices (overwhelmingly favorable) in British and American periodicals on its publication. A.H. Clough reported in June, 1852, that the *Memoirs* was one of the "two most circulating books of the [British] libraries I think" ("To Ralph Waldo Emerson," June 17, 1852, Letter 10, *Emerson-Clough Letters*, ed. Howard F. Lowry and Ralph L. Rusk [n.p.: Archon Books, 1968], n. pag.). As late as 1857 the *Memoirs* was still carried by Mudie's Circulating Library. *Woman* was well reviewed in the American press in 1845, but scantily and mostly unfavorably in the British, both in 1845 and

again in 1855, when it was reprinted. See Joel Myerson, *Margaret Fuller: An Annotated Secondary Bibliography* (New York: Burt Franklin, 1977).

[5]For example, James Russell Lowell's satire in his "A Fable for Critics" (1848) and Nathaniel Hawthorne's malicious comments in his *Italian Notebooks* (published posthumously by his son, Julian, in 1884).

[6]A.G.K. L'Estrange, *The Life of Mary Russell Mitford* (New York, 1870), II, 309-10.

[7]"E.B.B. to R.B.," January 4, 1860, Letter 190; "E.B.B. to R.B.," August 15, 1846, Letter 501, *The Letters of Robert Browning and Elizabeth Barrett Browning, 1845-1846*, ed. Elvan Kintner (Cambridge, Mass.: Belknap Press of Harvard Univ. Press, 1969), I, 361, and II, 961; "To Miss Mitford," September 24, 1850, *The Letters of Elizabeth Barrett Browning*, ed. Frederic G. Kenyon (New York, 1899), I, 459-60.

[8]"Margaret Fuller and Mary Wollstonecraft," rpt. Thomas Pinney, ed., *Essays of George Eliot* (New York: Columbia Univ. Press, 1963), p. 200; Gordon S. Haight, ed., *The George Eliot Letters*, Vol. II (New Haven: Yale Univ. Press, 1954), pp. 15, 48.

[9]"Margaret Fuller and Mary Wollstonecraft," in Pinney, *Essays*, p. 205.

[10]Elizabeth Cady Stanton, Susan B. Anthony, and Matilda Joslyn Gage, eds., *History of Woman Suffrage* (New York, 1881), I, 801, 802.

[11]Kate Sanborn, "Margaret Fuller (Marchioness D'Ossoli)" in *Our Famous Women. An Authorized Record of Their Lives and Deeds* (Hartford, Conn., 1884), p. 297.

[12]On the fictional madwoman, see Sandra Gilbert and Susan Gubar, *The Madwoman in the Attic: The Woman Writer and the Nineteenth Century Imagination* (New Haven: Yale Univ. Press, 1979). Ann Douglas argues that Fuller saw her life in terms of history, not fiction; see "Margaret Fuller and the Search for History: A Biographical Study," *Women's Studies*, 4 (1976), 37-86.

[13]*Memoirs*, I, 10-11.

[14]Fuller, *Woman in the Nineteenth Century* (1845; rpt. New York: W.W. Norton, 1971), pp. 38-41 [15-179]. Later references will be incorporated into the text.

[15]See, for example, W.H. Channing in *Memoirs*, II, 173, and R.W. Emerson, *Memoirs*, I, 287. Perry Miller discusses the widespread identification of Fuller with Mme. de Staël and her heroine, Corinne, the romantic woman of genius, in *Margaret Fuller: American Romantic. A Selection from Her Writings and Correspondence* (1963; rpt. Ithaca, N.Y.: Cornell Univ. Press, 1970), pp. xviii-xxiv. See also, on the enormous influence of *Corinne* on women generally in the nineteenth century, Ellen Moers, *Literary Women* (Garden City, N.Y.: Anchor Press/Doubleday, 1977), pp. 263-319.

[16]On Fuller as an inspiration, see, for example, Sarah Freeman Clarke, in Thomas Wentworth Higginson, *Margaret Fuller Ossoli* (Boston, 1895), pp. 117-18; on Fuller as freak, see James Russell Lowell's character Miranda in "A Fable for Critics," *Poetical Works of James Russell Lowell* (Boston: Houghton Mifflin, 1904), IV, 62-64.

[17]Gamaliel Bradford depicts Fuller as becoming a True Woman in *Portraits of American Women* (Boston: Houghton Mifflin, 1919), p. 162; see also *Westminster Review*, 67 (1852). Nathaniel Hawthorne has particularly unkind things to say about Fuller's sexual behavior in his *Italian Notebooks*; see *The Portable Hawthorne*, ed. Malcolm Cowley (New York: Viking, 1948), pp. 594-97.

[18]"To Mrs. Jameson," February 26, 1852; "To Miss Mitford," September 24, 1850, *Letters of Elizabeth Barrett Browning*, ed. Kenyon, II, 59; I, 459-60.

¹⁹Margaret Fuller Ossoli, *At Home and Abroad, or Things and Thoughts in America and Europe*, ed. Arthur B. Fuller (1856; rpt. Port Washington, N.Y.: Kennikat, 1971), p. 320.

²⁰Chevigny, pp. 382–83, 394–95, argues this interpretation.

Chapter 4

¹The studies of Victoria which best reflect her complexities are Elizabeth Longford's *Victoria RI* (London: Weidenfeld and Nicholson, 1964), and Cecil Woodham-Smith's *Queen Victoria: Her Life and Times, 1819–1861* (London: Hamish Hamilton, 1972).

²*Dearest Child: Letters between Queen Victoria and the Princess Royal, 1858–1861*, ed. Roger Fulford (New York: Holt, 1964), p. 112.

³Journal for October 14–5, 1839, quoted by Woodham-Smith, p. 184.

⁴Journal for February 10, 1840, quoted by Woodham-Smith, p. 205.

⁵Journal for February 28, 1840, quoted by Longford, p. 148.

⁶Journal for November 3, 1844, quoted by Longford, p. 174.

⁷Journal for July 6, 1849, quoted by Longford, p. 212.

⁸*Letters of Queen Victoria*, ed. Hector Bolitho (New Haven: Yale Univ. Press, 1938), p. 26. The Melbourne quotation is from Victoria's Journal for October 14, 1839, quoted by Longford, p. 133.

⁹*The Letters of Queen Victoria*, ed. A.C. Benson and Viscount Esher (New York: Longmans, 1907), II, pp. 438, 444.

¹⁰Mrs. Sarah Stickney Ellis, *The Wives of England* (London, 1843); quotation from Longford, p. 569.

¹¹*Letters*, ed. Bolitho, p. 109.

¹²Ibid., pp. 119–20, 120, 143, 152, 153.

¹³Quoted by Sir Theodore Martin in *Queen Victoria as I Knew Her* (Edinburgh: Blackwood, 1908), pp. 69–70.

¹⁴Gladstone's note and Victoria's reply appear in Philip Guedalla's *The Queen and Mr. Gladstone* (Garden City, N.Y.: Doubleday, 1934), p. 266.

¹⁵Quoted in ibid., pp. 271, 272. Dr. Mary E. Walker was an American who drew particularly sharp criticism because of her insistence upon her right not only to enter the male profession of medicine but also to adopt the male prerogative of trousers.

¹⁶Quoted by Frank Hardie, *The Political Influence of Queen Victoria* (London: Oxford, 1935), p. 140.

¹⁷Longford, p. 234. For recent work on Victoria and childbirth, see Adrienne Rich's "The Theft of Childbirth" *The New York Review of Books*, October 2, 1975, pp. 25–30, and John Hawkins Miller's "Temple and Sewer: Childbirth, Prudery, and Victoria Regina" in *The Victorian Family*, ed. A.S. Wohl (London: Croom Helm, 1978), pp. 23–43.

¹⁸Ibid., p. 395.

¹⁹Journal for October 10, 1839, quoted by Woodham-Smith, p. 182.

²⁰Journal for October 11–14, 1839, quoted by Woodham-Smith, pp. 183.

²¹*Dearest Child*, pp. 77–78. Later references will be incorporated into the text.

²²*Letters*, ed. Bolitho, p. 120.

²³Dearest Child, pp. 99, 150.

Chapter 5

[1]"Of Queens' Gardens" was delivered as a lecture on December 14, 1864, and published in *Sesame and Lilies* in 1865.

[2]Walter Houghton calls it "the most important single document I know for the characteristic idealization of love, woman, and the home in Victorian society." See *The Victorian Frame of Mind, 1830–1870* (New Haven: Yale Univ. Press, 1957), p. 343n. Kate Millett similarly takes the essay as representative of conservative attitudes when she contrasts Ruskin's reactionary sentimentalism with John Stuart Mill's radical egalitarianism; see her *Sexual Politics* (Garden City, N.Y.: Doubleday, 1970), pp. 88–108. David Sonstroem attacks Millett's reading of Ruskin, emphasizing Ruskin's larger social aims, in "Millett versus Ruskin: A Defense of Ruskin's 'Of Queens' Gardens,'" *Victorian Studies*, 20 (1977), 283–97.

[3]See *The Winnington Letters: John Ruskin's Correspondence with Margaret Alexis Bell and the Children at Winnington Hall*, ed. Van Akin Burd (Cambridge, Mass.: Harvard Univ. Press, 1969).

[4]Derek Hudson, *Munby: Man of Two Worlds. The Life and Diaries of Arthur J. Munby, 1828–1910* (London: Gambit, 1972), p. 177. On February 5, 1864, Munby attended an organizational meeting for the Working Women's College and reported "a letter from Ruskin who in his wild way vetoes the whole thing."

[5]"Of Queens' Gardens," *Sesame and Lilies* (London, 1865; rpt. London: J.M. Dent, 1970), pp. 49–50 [48–79]. Later references will be incorporated into the text.

[6]The names refer to Wordsworth's "Lucy" poems about a child of nature (whose name means light) who dies still young and innocent; to Tennyson's "Maud," another shining child-woman, worshipped from afar by her tormented lover, who comes out of and returns to the crueler world outside Maud's garden; and to the Biblical Magdalen or Madeleine (for which "Maud" is of course a short form of the common English pronunciation). The Magdalen is a woman of the world, herself once a prostitute (according to the prevalent nineteenth-century reading of the Gospels), who in her reformed life can become a model for the socially responsible woman willing to leave the domestic garden and work to turn the rest of the world into a garden, too.

[7]Quoted by Roger B. Stein, *John Ruskin and Aesthetic Thought in America, 1840–1900* (Cambridge, Mass.: Harvard Univ. Press, 1967), p. 263. The publication figures for America are also from Stein, p. 226; those for Great Britain are from *The Works of John Ruskin*, Library Edition, ed. E.T. Cook and Alexander Wedderburn (London: George Allen, 1903–12), III and XVIII.

[8][R. Sturgis, Jr.], "Ruskin's *Sesame and Lilies*," *North American Review*, 102 (1866), 310–11 [306–12].

[9][Anne Mozley], "Educators," *Blackwood's*, 78 (1865), 754.

[10]"*Sesame and Lilies*," *Saturday Review*, 20 (1865), 83.

[11]Anthony Trollope, "*Sesame and Lilies*," *Fortnightly*, 1 (1865), 633, 635 [633–635].

[12][John R. de C. Wise], "Contemporary Literature—Belles Lettres," *Westminster Review*, 84 (1865), 574, 575.

[13]"Of Kings' Treasuries," *Sesame and Lilies*, pp. 28–29.

[14]"*Sesame and Lilies*," *Saturday Review*, 20 (1865), 84.

[15]"Mr. Ruskin on Books and Women," *Victoria Magazine*, 6 (1865), 131–33.

[16]Ibid., pp. 136–37.

[17]John Stuart Mill, *The Subjection of Women* (London, 1869; rpt. in *Essays on Sex Equality*, ed. Alice Rossi [Chicago: Univ. of Chicago Press, 1970]), p. 167.

[18]Ibid., pp. 238–39.

Chapter 6

[1]George Somes Layard, *Mrs. Lynn Linton: Her Life, Letters, and Opinions* (London: Methuen, 1901), pp. 35–36. Later references will be incorporated into the text.

[2]Algernon Charles Swinburne, *The Complete Works of Algernon Charles Swinburne*, ed. Sir Edmund Gosse and Thomas James Wise (London: Heinemann, 1925), VI, 287–88.

[3]Quoted by Mrs. Alec Tweedie, "A Chat with Mrs. Lynn Linton," *Temple Bar*, 102 (1894), 360 [355–64]. For other late pieces by and about Linton, see her "Candour in English Fiction," *New Review*, 2 (1890), 10–14, and "Literature: Then and Now," *Fortnightly*, 53 (1890), 517–31, plus Helen C. Black's chapter on Linton in *Notable Women Authors of the Day* (Glasgow, 1893), pp. 1–10, and the responses to her death, particularly "Mrs. Lynn Linton," *Athenaeum*, 3691 (1898), 131–32, and Beatrice Harraden's "Mrs. Lynn Linton" in *The Bookman*, 8 (1898), 16–17.

[4]"The Modern Revolt," *Macmillan's*, 23 (1871), 149 [142–49].

[5]Linton's "Modern Mothers" appeared in *Saturday Review*, 25 (1868), 269 [268–69]. Gail Cunningham links Linton's 1868 attacks on the Girl of the Period and her 1895 attacks on the New Woman in *The New Woman and the Victorian Novel* (London: Macmillan, 1978), pp. 8–15.

[6]"An Appeal to Fashionable Mothers," *Victoria*, 10 (1868), 537 [537–38].

[7]Eliza Lynn Linton, "The Girl of the Period," *Saturday Review*, 25 (1868), 339–40; rpt. *Living Age* 97 (1868), 188–90; the essay first appeared under Linton's name in *The Girl of the Period and Other Social Essays* (London, 1883).

[8]There has been very little work done on Linton herself. Vineta Colby discusses her largely as a novelist (*The Singular Anomaly* [New York: New York Univ. Press, 1970]), pp. 15–45; Duncan Crow devotes part of a chapter to the Girl of the Period (G.O.P.) controversy (*The Victorian Woman* [London: Allen & Unwin, 1971]), pp. 190–98. Neither Crow nor Colby, however, goes beyond Layard in the information they present or the analyses they make of the G.O.P.

[9]Merle Mowbray Bevington, *The Saturday Review, 1855–1868* (New York: Columbia, 1941), p. 110.

[10]Ibid., p. 112.

[11]Black, p. 4.

[12]J.B. Mayor, "The Cry of the Women," *Contemporary Review* 11 (1869), 201–02 [196–215].

[13]"The Girl of the Period," *Victoria* 11 (1868), 469.

[14]"Affairs in England," *New York Times*, August 27, 1868, p. 5. On p. 2 of the August 26, 1869, issue, the paper discussed M.E. Braddon's "Whose Fault Is It?" which had appeared in *Belgravia* in July, pp. 214–16.

[15]"The Paradox of the Period," *Tomahawk*, 2 (1868), 202; "the ordinary mutton-chop of the period" is from "Ourselves," *Blackwood's*, 108 (1870), 177; "The Cigar of the Period" is advertized in Bernand's *The Girls of the Period* (London, 1809). "The Poetry of the Period" is the name which *Temple Bar* gave to its poetry

review section as of July, 1869; "The Reviewer of the Period," *Judy*, 2 (1868), 288; "The Shakespeare of the Period," *Tomahawk*, 4 (1869), 154; "A Wife of the Period," *Harper's*, 38 (1868–69), 378–86; "A School-Girl of the Period," *Harper's*, 39 (1869), 674; "The Children of the Period," *Punch*, 55 (1868), 268; "The Roman Girl of the Period," *Belgravia*, 12 (1870), 301–06; "The Girl of the Future," *Victoria*, 15 (1870), 440–47, 491–502; "Daimona, The Dangerous Woman of the Period," *Southern Magazine*, 10 (1872), 331–41; "The Past and Future of the Girl of the Period," *London Society*, 16 (1869), 463–67; "Puffs of the Period," *Punch*, 57 (1869), 5. *The Girl of the Period Miscellany* and *Almanac* appeared in 1869 (London), edited by "Miss Echo"; the *Songster* was issued in New York the same year; Alfred Austin, *The Poetry of the Period* (London, 1870).

[16]*Tomahawk*, 5 (1869), 116.

[17]"The Joke of the Period," *Tomahawk*, 4 (1869), 34. "Since . . ." is from *Judy*, 2 (1868), 304. Among many other one-liners are: "In the *Saturday Review* of the 14th ult., for 'The Girl of the Period' read 'The Girl of the *Periodical*'" (*Fun*, 7 [1868], 38); "THE GIRL OF THE PERIOD.—Example of 'locus a non lucendo'—a girl who is too fast to mind her proper stops" (*Tomahawk*, 2 [1868], 153); "PRESENTS FOR A GIRL OF THE PERIOD.—A bottle of olives, and a box of cigars" (*Punch*, 56 [1869], 32).

[18]"AN APROPOS SOLILOQUY," *Tomahawk*, 4 (1869), 46. For other poems see *Judy*'s "The Reviewer of the Period," plus "Women's Emancipation," *Tomahawk*, 2 (1868), 134; "A Saturday's Review," *Fun*, 7 (1868), 68; "The Girl (Not) of the Period," *Fun*, 7 (1868), 129.

[19]F.C. Bernand, *The Girls of the Period; or, The Island of Nowarpartickilar. A Folly* (London, 1869). For other dramatic pieces, see "The Girl of the Period," *Fun*, 7 (1868), 49; "Mrs. Punch's Letters to Her Daughter," *Punch*, 55 (1868), 143; "Amusement for the People," *Tomahawk*, 3 (1868), 24; "Ballet of the Period," *Punch*, 56 (1869), 79; "The Period," *Fun*, 9 (1869), 214.

[20]"'Look at the Clock,'" *Punch*, 56 (1869), 3; "*The Saturday Shrew*," *Fun*, 9 (1869), 81. For other sharp pieces, see *Fun*'s "Our Fun-Done Letter," 7 (1868), 44; "Pot and Kettle," 9 (1869), 138; "Girls of the Period," 9 (1869), 187.

[21]Eliza Lynn Linton, "Costume and Its Morals," *Saturday Review*, 24 (1867), 44–45. The clothes controversy was part of the larger concern with women's health and morals in the 1860s. See "Science," Volume II, Chapter 2 and "Passionate Heroines: Fallen, Sensation and Fleshly," Volume III, Chapter 4.

[22]"The Girl and the Period," *Tomahawk*, 2 (1868), 174–75; [Edward Dicey] "The Women of the Day," *St. Paul's Magazine*, 2 (1868), 311 [302–18]; "The Past and Future Girl . . . ," p. 463.

[23]For some of the best early replies to the *Saturday Review*, see "Woman and Her Critics," *Tomahawk*, 2 (1868), 72; "The 'Saturday Sneerer's' View of English Girls," *Judy*, 2 (1868), 297; *Tomahawk*'s "The Girl and the Period"; and "American Ladies v. English," *Judy*, 3 (1868), 2.

[24]The *Fun* illustration was titled "A Reflection" and appeared on May 9, 1868, p. 100. *Tomahawk* and *Judy* followed with illustrations on January 23 and 27 of 1869 ("The Young Gentleman[!] of the Day," pp. 36–37, and "The Young Man of the Period," p. 139). For the *Punch* letter, see "Mrs. Punch's Letters to Her Daughter" (55 [1868], 180); the *Judy* poem appeared on January 20, 1869, p. 130. The Young Man of the Period spawned at least two quips. "'The Coming Man.'—A Waiter," *Punch*, 57 (1869), 91. "HOW THE BOY OF THE PERIOD 'DOES' XENOPHON—'πζροζγ éis Expedeis'—they walked into the Sardines,"

Tomahawk, 4 (1869), 107. The Young Man struck back, not, significantly, at women, but at fathers, by drafting "The Old Man of the Period," *Fun*, 8 (1869), 200. Finally, there is Samuel Bracebridge Hemyng's *The Man of the Period* (London, 1870).

[25]Mayors, pp. 202, 204.

[26]Agnes T. Harrison's "Two Girls of the Period" appeared initially in *Macmillan's*, 19 (1869), 323–39, and was immediately reprinted in *Living Age* (100 [1869], 605–17). Henry James's "Modern Women" (*Nation*, 7 [1868], 332–34) reviews *Modern Women and What Is Said of Them* (New York, 1868), an anonymously published collection of *Saturday Review* articles written by Linton and J.R. Green; the quotation from James's review is from p. 333. Later quotations from this review will be incorporated into the text. For other responses to this volume, see "Modern Women," *Atlantic Monthly*, 22 (1868), 639–40; "Modern Women," *Ladies' Repository*, 28 (1868), 396; "Modern Women," *Putnam's Magazine*, 2 (1868), 754–55; "Modern Views About Women," *Tinsley's Magazine*, 5 (1870), 660–64. For responses to Linton's other collection of *Saturday Review* essays, *Ourselves* (London, 1869), see "Ourselves," *Athenaeum*, 2182 (1869), 236–37; "Essays on Women," *Pall Mall Gazette*, 10 (1869), 116, rpt. *Living Age*, 103 (1869), 262–65; "Ourselves," *Blackwood's*, 108 (1870), 173–77. For other serious responses to the G.O.P. controversy and problem, see [Howard Williams] "Women and Their Satirists," *Temple Bar*, 24 (1868), 555–69; "Modern Characteristics," *Victoria*, 12 (1869), 230–40; "Fine Ladies and Good Housewives," *Once A Week*, 3 (1869), 30–32; [Montagu Burrows] "Female Education," *Quarterly Review*, 126 (1869), 448–79; "Women's Education," *Fraser's Magazine*, 79 (1869), 537–52; "Women: Past, Present, and Future," *English Domestic Magazine*, 17 (1870), 219–20; Charles Kingsley, "Nausicaa in London; or, The Lower Education of Women," *Good Words for 1874*, ed. D. Macleod (London, 1874), pp. 18–23, rpt. in Kingsley's *Sanitary and Social Essays and Lectures* (London, 1880), pp. 107–27.

[27]Braddon, p. 214.

[28]"The Latest Crusade," *Victoria*, 11 (1868), [193–201] 199–200. The *St. Paul's* essay which *Victoria* attacks is "The Women of the Day."

Index

11–12; as only source of political morality, 12–13; dependent upon purity and isolation, 12–13; as guiding image, 80

responses to: 13–14. *See also* Marion Reid

Linton, Eliza Lynn

life: crisis of faith, 103–04; paradoxical character, 104; John Douglas Cook, 105–06; journalistic and novelistic success, 106; late popularity, 106

as controversialist: best work criticizes society effectively, 107–08, 133nn3, 4, 5, 134n21

"The Girl of the Period": ideal of the "fair young English girl," 108; the "Girl of the Period" and purity of taste, 109; and demi-mondains, 109–10; and loveless materialistic marriages, 110–11; male reaction against, 111–12; bibliographical data, 133n7, 135n26

G.O.P. controversy: scope, 113–14; offspring—expressions, 114–15; jokes, verse plays, 115–17; essays, 117

G.O.P. issues: what is not involved, 112–13; context, 117–18; Linton accused of not recognizing the economic forces affecting marriage and courtship (J.B. Mayors), 118–19; Linton accused of exaggerating women's foibles and of ignoring male influence, 119; Henry James's response— general criticism, 119–20; contrast of the G.O.P. and the American Girl, 120; attacks Linton's lack of sympathy with the economic plight of young women, 121; society's growing love of luxury, 122; woman as reflection of society's ills, 123; *Victoria* rejects *St. Paul's* paternalistic defense of woman, 123–25

modern work on: Layard, G., 133n1; Cunningham, G., 133n5; Colby, V. and Crow, D., 133n8; Bevington, M., 133n9, 133n10

Linton, William James, 104

Lucy (Wordsworth's), 83–84, 90

Macarthur, Mary, xiii

Macaulay, Thomas B., 129n4

Magdalen (Madeleine), 90, 95

man: claim to power, 11–12, 15, 36, 53–54; nature of, 11, 26–27, 35–36, 49–50, 59–60, 73, 74, 80–81, 118, 119

marriage: criticism of, 34, 44, 70–75, 99, 110–11; Fuller's, 44–45; ideal of, 62, 64–66, 78, 80–87, 86. *See also* slavery

Martin, Louis Aimé, 3

Martin, Sir Theodore, 67, 131n13

Martineau, Harriet, 5, 20

Maud (Tennyson's), 90, 95

influence of, 128n17
religion, 103–04; effects on women, 4, 7–8, 14, 15, 51–53, 55, 62, 85–86
Ricardo, David, 24
Rousseau, Jean Jacques, 3
Ruskin, John
  social and economic criticism, 77, 78, 97
  attitudes toward women: support of angelic ideal, 77, 81–82, 104; encouragement of as critics and social reformers, 77–78, 90–96, 104; woman's nature and abilities, 78, 81–82; women's education, 78–79, 82–89; women's social service, 78, 90–96; Rose La Touche, 79–80; women's work, 79
  "Of Queens' Gardens": as classic description of True Woman, 77; as Carlylesque social criticism, 77; on woman's nature —angelic, 77; complementary to men, 81; guiding and ruling, 81; presiding over home, 81–82; instinctively wise, 82; selfless, gentle, adaptable, 82; child of nature, 83–84, 86–87; like Wordsworth's Lucy, 83–84, 90; on women's education—support for improved, 78; physical, 83–84; preparation to sympathize with husband, 84, 86; imagination and sympathy, 85; dangers of theology, 85–86; as serious as boys', 86, 87; no restraints on, 86–87; no modern novels, 86; the arts, 87; moral, 87; teachers, 88, exposure to nature, 88; *Victoria Magazine* on, 99–100; on women's social responsibilities—"queenly power," 78, 80, 91, 92; public work or duties, 90–96; as Tennyson's Maud, 90, 95; as Madeleine or Magdalen, 90, 95; need to leave walled garden, 91, 93–95; as Lady or "bread-giver," 92; as Regina or "Right-doer," 92; as Dante's Matilda, 95; *Victoria Magazine* on, 100–01; Mill on, 101–02
  contemporary responses to "Of Queens' Gardens": popularity of, 96; attacks on—*Blackwood's*, 96; *Saturday Review*, 97, 98; Trollope (*Fortnightly*), 97; *Victoria Magazine*, 99–100; praise for—*Westminster*, 97; *Victoria Magazine*, 100–01; Mill's *Subjection* and, 101–02
  "Of Kings' Treasuries," 96, 98
  art criticism, 97
  modern work on: Houghton, W., Millett, K., Sonstroem, D., 132n1; Burd, V.A., 132n3; Stein, R.B., Cook, E.T., Wedderburn, A., 132n7
Saint-Simon, Count Claude de, 24, 52

pathetic pleasures, 30–31

Appeal as political argument: women need equal civil rights, 31–32; these rights assured only through equal political rights—need the protection of equal laws, 5, 32–33; need to participate in the choice of legislators to acquire and protect these laws, 33–34; need the expansion of mind resulting from life and interests beyond home, 34–35

Appeal as economic argument: woman so enslaved by despotic economic situation that Competition must be replaced by Cooperation—how woman's physical size and child-bearing role prevent her from competing for equal wages and benefits, 35–36; how cooperation would free woman to contribute what she can and receive what she needs, 36–37; how the first step toward this economic revolution must be equal civil and political rights, 37, 78

modern work on: Pankhurst, R.K.P., 129nn2, 3, 5, 7; Ramelson, M., Rover, C., Rowbotham, S., 129n2

Transcendentalism, 39

Trollope, Anthony, 97, 120

Tweedie, Mrs. Alec, 133n3

Utilitarian Society, 25

Utilitarianism, 6, 22, 23, 24

Victoria, Princess Royal (Vicky), 63, 65, 70, 71, 75

Victoria, Queen

early life: death of father, attachment to father-surrogates, 64

conventional aspects: need for Albert as guide and educator, 64, 65–66; need to serve Albert and children as wife-mother, 64–66; mourning, 66–67; anti-feminist—"Women's Rights," 67–68; women doctors, especially Dr. Mary Walker, 68–69

unconventional aspects: as "feminist" influence—example for apocalyptic feminists, 58–59, 62; for career-minded women, 69; anesthesia during child-birth, 69–70; sexually—strong physical attraction to Albert, 70; sees marriage as enslaving, 70, 73–74; pregnancy as miserable, 71–72; young babies as unattractive, 72; men as selfish and predatory, 73–74; Albert as "mother," 44, 64, 75

modern work on: Longford, E., 69, 131nn1, 5, 6, 7, 8, 17; Woodham-Smith, C., 131nn1, 3, 4, 19, 20; Fulford, R., 131n2; Bolitho, H., 131nn8, 11, 22; Benson, A. and Viscount Esher, 131n9; Guedalla, P., 131n14; Hardie, F., 131n15; Miller, J., 131n17; Rich, A., 131n17

APR 28